I WISH FOR CHANGE

I WISH FOR CHANGE

Unleashing the Power of Kids to
Make a Difference

By Kyle Schwartz

Da Capo

LIFE
LONG

Da Capo Press
Hachette Book Group
1290 Avenue of the Americas, New York, NY 10104
www.dacapopress.com
@DaCapoPress

Printed in the United States of America

First Edition: July 2019

Published by Da Capo Press, an imprint of Perseus Books, LLC,
a subsidiary of Hachette Book Group, Inc.

The Hachette Speakers Bureau provides a wide range of authors for speaking events. To find out more, go to www.hachettespeakersbureau.com or call (866) 376-6591.

The publisher is not responsible for websites (or their content) that are not owned by the publisher.

Editorial production by Lori Hobkirk at the Book Factory.
Print book interior design by Cynthia Young at Sagecraft.

Library of Congress Cataloging-in-Publication Data has been applied for.

ISBNs: 978-0-7382-8563-4 (paper over board); 978-0-7382-8564-1 (ebook)

10   9   8   7   6   5   4   3   2   1

*I would like to dedicate this book to
every young person with an ambition
to make a difference. I know there will be a day
when your wishes become reality.*

Contents

Author's Note

I Wish for Change wouldn't exist without the hundreds of children that I've had the pleasure to teach. Their stories are what make this book come alive. To protect the privacy of my students and their families, certain identifying characteristics have been changed.

Introduction

I Wish for Change

I wish for the world to be in peace and for there to be no wars.

The best part of writing a book focused on youth empowerment has been the opportunity to get to know so many young people who are already making a difference in their communities. Their stories have been a constant source of encouragement and inspiration. As I spoke with them, I noticed similar themes coming up in each of our conversations. I decided to explore this further and conducted a little thought experiment. I invited a few of the young people featured in this book to help out by simply asking them to finish the sentence: *Most adults think young people are* _____.

Here are some of their responses:

"irresponsible"

"incapable"

"unmotivated"

"lazy"

I can't say I am surprised to hear that young people, even those who are already deeply engaged their community, think this is the shared perception of adults. A common narrative seems to be that young people of today are somehow worse than the generations that came before. Author Richie Norton points out that Google auto completes the phrase "Millennials are . . ." with the terms "lazy," "stupid," "idiots," "the worst," "entitled," and "killing the napkin industry." So many of the young people I talked with feel discounted and dismissed by adults as a whole.

I wanted to dig a little deeper into how adults actually see young people. So, I continued this thought experiment on social media. I asked adults to complete the sentence: "Most young people are _____." Here are some responses I received:

"a joy to be around"

"more resilient than we give them credit for"

"inventive, imaginative, full of energy, and optimistic"

"full of stories worth writing"

"an endless supply of energy, raw ideas, and promise"

Perhaps these particular respondents had a different perception of young people than the majority of adults. Or perhaps the type of adults who make negative generalizations about youth were not compelled to put those thoughts in writing. Or maybe there is a dramatic disconnect between the views that most adults hold about young people and what we communicate. Could it be that most adults actually think positively about young people but just don't express it?

Young people are clearly listening when grown-ups drone on and on about "kids these days." They hear the same recycled lines about the younger generation not being prepared for the "real world." They are subject to endless hand-wringing about the ills of social media, an over reliance on technology, and a need to be constantly rewarded. My sixteen-year-old cousin Colin left his traditional school and opted to take his high school classes online. His central rationale was, "My teachers were always putting us down. They say we are lazy and always on our phones. I just got sick of it. I don't want to be stuck in a room all day with people who hate my entire generation." Colin told me there are, indeed, supportive adults in his life, particularly his parents, but on the whole the constant criticism from adults is, "Bad and getting worse."

When I told Colin I was writing this book, he was instantly encouraging. He said he was proud of me, that the topic was important, and that he couldn't wait to read it. His pep talk was exactly what I needed to keep me going. It broke my heart to think that Colin may not hear the same motivating messages from adults that he so freely gives.

Do young people like Colin ever hear a counter narrative? Do they know there are adults who champion their potential? Do they hear us rooting for them? Or is it drowned out by a million little sighs, slights, and eye rolls?

As caring adults, we must aim for encouragement to be louder than all the negativity. This book seeks to be the antidote to the intergenerational mudslinging, to serve as a reminder of the influence we can have on young people. After all, the successes of young people are shared by us all. We all benefit when a young person sees a problem and takes action. Children can make a difference, not years from now, not when they are older, but right now. Why wait?

Have you ever asked a child why they are in school? As a third-grade teacher, I ask this question to my students each year. Their answers seem to follow a script. Almost every child will answer confidently that they go to school so they can learn. If you ask a child why they need to learn, many will tell you it's so they can get good grades. Then, they might add, they will need good grades in order to go to college or so they can get a good job.

This thinking is so prevalent that it is rarely challenged. Workforce training, while certainly a benefit of schooling, is not the goal of education. My students are learning to read, write, and multiply not so they can ace a test or snag a job, but because those skills will help them navigate and understand the world. I tell my students, "You are not here so you can make money in a decade. You are here so you can make a difference now." The obligation of the school is to teach, but the obligation of the student is to contribute.

Young people are up for the task. While my generation was, in the words of singer-songwriter John Mayer, "Waiting on the world to change," the children of today are not so complacent. They are changing the world right now. This book is filled with the stories of real, young people who have already helped others, who have already made a difference. This is a side of children I am very familiar with.

I work with young people day in and day out. I don't often witness deeply ingrained selfishness and egocentrism. More often than not, I see organized efforts to help others alongside small acts of compassion. Kids in my class have raised money to send goats and chickens to children in need halfway around the world. They have collected canned foods for the local homeless shelter, even though 90 percent of the students at my school live below or very near the poverty line. One year, our soccer team hosted a

I wish that there was more Peace on earth...
For Example

• Less littering
• Less Smoking
• Less homless
• Less poor
• Less bad People
• More good People

Please help more People!

yard sale on the front lawn of our school and donated all the pro-
ceeds to a local animal shelter. Our students have sent handmade
cards to the veterans hospital on Veterans Day and to the senior
center on Valentine's Day.

It's these everyday acts of casual kindness that reveal my students' true nature. When I knock something over in my classroom, a child is there helping me clean it up, before I even have a
chance to bend down. When a child scrapes their knee at recess, a
group of kids rushes over to prop them up. They tie each other's
shoes, pick up litter, and present me with an endless stream of
drawings and crafts. When a child makes a teary-eyed confession
to the class that they have lost someone they love, the other children scoot closer to put a loving arm around a friend's shoulder.
They offer words of comfort and encouragement. These acts of
generosity add up.

I saw firsthand the impact my students can make when I asked
them to write notes to me starting with the phrase "I wish my

teacher knew." Their answers were thoughtful and honest. One said, "I wish my teacher knew I don't have pencils at home to do my homework." Another said, "I wish my teacher knew how much I love my family."

Photographs of the notes went viral. In doing so, my students inspired teachers from Algeria to Japan to Germany to ask the same beautifully humble question, "What do you wish your teacher knew?" Their voices were featured on every major media outlet from the *Today Show* to the *Today Show Australia*, and *Good Morning America* to *Good Morning Great Britain*.

What did my students do with all the fervor and excitement of being on television? One girl came to school with an idea. "Miss, we are famous now!" she proclaimed. I figured the next line might be a plea to cancel homework, but instead she finished, "So we should help people." This suggestion started a modest neighborhood effort to collect books, which later became a citywide book drive sponsored by our local television station. We collected and distributed tens of thousands of books to families all across the city of Denver.

In writing this book, I confirmed that my students are not an exception to the rule; they are merely one example among many. Young people of all ages, backgrounds, and lifestyles are actively making their communities better. I am honored to share some of their stories. In reading their accomplishments, I hope you realize that each of these young people had the guidance and support of adults just like us. We can be the caring adults who believe in the potential in every child and are ready to step up and help them make a difference.

Each chapter in this book explores a different aspect of empowerment, from understanding power and fairness to the importance of belonging, effort, responsibility, and agency. In addition to inspiring stories, each chapter also shows through anecdotes and research why young people are so effective at improving the world.

At the end of each chapter, you'll find a section called "Spark the Conversation." It offers open-ended questions that you can use to start a dialogue with the young people in your life. Teachers can start these conversations with their students, families can open up a dialogue with their own children, and coaches can explore empowerment with their players. Having these conversations is just one of the many actionable steps you can take to empower young people. I hope this book leaves you with tips and strategies to show children how powerful their voices, choices, and passions truly are.

Right now, young people all over the globe are solving problems they didn't create. Children are not responsible for issues such as war, housing insecurity, global warming, and inequities in education, yet so many are willing to work toward solutions. We need the wisdom, creativity, and leadership of young people. The more young people feel empowered to make a difference, the sooner we all will be living in the better world that these young people are wishing for.

The question is this: Will you help young people turn their wishes into reality?

I Wish

I wish that there was no more sicknesses.

1

Understanding the "Power" in Empowerment

> I wish everyone in the world had /has education.

Are my students empowered?

I would like the answer to this question to be a simple, complete "Yes." But in order to know if my students are empowered, I need to understand what empowerment is. Easy enough, right?

Well, it turns out empowerment is one of those deceptive little words. It seems straight forward but hides a multitude of theories and philosophies inside it. There is no unanimously agreed-upon definition, so we each get to form the meaning of empowerment ourselves. To do that we must understand "power."

We all live in a world made up of a complex, layered web of social norms, societal pressures, and ingrained power structures. If we want the young people in our lives to not only be able to navigate this world, but also to challenge it and improve it, we must help them explore the concept of power.

> I wish that everyone is treated equal.

Is Power Good or Bad?

Jennifer Bacon, community organizer and member of the Denver Board of Education, wisely stressed that people who have been disenfranchised and abused by systems such as government or education often see power as both negative and fixed. "It is like a learned powerlessness," Bacon explains. "When your perception changes and you see power as neutral, you reset the power structure. You can claim a collective power. Only then can you work toward change."

Most social scientists define power as the capacity to influence others. While that definition of power is decidedly neutral, the effect of influencing others can often make people view power either positively or negatively.

If, as a teacher, I say, "I'm in total control of my classroom," that may be viewed as a boastful statement of my skills as an educator. But if a student in my classroom said, "My teacher has total control over me," we would assume that child feels insignificant.

If we want to be empowered and empower others, we must conceive of power as relational rather than dominant in nature. We shouldn't teach young people to fear or avoid power. We should teach young people to embrace power and cultivate it through coalition.

That's what Milo Cress did. He was just nine years old when he noticed something at restaurants. Milo realized that nearly every drink was automatically served with a plastic straw, and he figured all those straws were going to end up in the trash. Milo wanted to change that.

"I was worried adults wouldn't listen to me because I was a kid . . . but I found the opposite to be true." Milo told a reporter for the *Daily Beast*. Milo took his fantastically simple idea—an "offer first policy"—to his local café, and the management agreed to offer customers a straw first instead of just popping them in drinks. "Initially, I just was annoyed at the waste," Milo explained. "I started talking to some other people, some of my friends, and convinced them to order drinks without straws." Milo told me what started as just talking to people close to him about ways they could reduce their own personal waste soon turned into more people wanting to reduce their use of single-use plastic straws.

From there, Milo created the organization Be Straw Free in order to continue advocating for this change. He encourages young people to use the "Each One Reach One" strategy, which he describes this way: "Each person invites (at least) one restaurant to consider offering straws to customers instead of serving a straw with each drink automatically." He also encourages customers to order drinks without straws whenever they don't need or want to use one. Now cafés and restaurants around the world, even global companies such as Starbucks, McDonalds, Disney, and several airlines, are turning away from single-use plastic straws.

This is a perfect example of the power of relationships. Milo started with a small action he could personally take. He reached out to his friends, family, and the local business community to convince them to do the same. Then he helped those people leverage their relationships to advocate for change.

Adults tell young people, "One person can change the world." That statement is true, but it stops short. Instead, we should tell children, "One person can change the world when they get a lot of other people to work alongside them." Our messaging to young people needs be "leverage your relationships, embrace your influence, and use it responsibly."

I wish that people would stop polluting the ocean because I love turtles and sea life.

Seeing the Culture of Power

Third-grade math is all about multiplication. Kids love it. They see multiplication as a special knowledge reserved for "the big kids" and are eager to join the club. One of my students' favorite lessons is called "Array Day." I show them examples of arrays—objects organized into columns and rows—and then I look both ways and whisper as if I am revealing a secret, "You all are living inside an array, and you don't know it." I pull back a little and cautiously explain, "You are all sitting in an array right now." The kids glance at each other, and there is a communal gasp as they realize that for most of their lives they have been organized into neat columns and rows on colorful classroom rugs.

Armed with a clipboard and a worksheet, I send them off to find examples of arrays in the real world. There is a collective awakening as they realize their entire world is filled with arrays. The calendar on the wall . . . array! Tiles on the floor . . . array! Tables in the cafeteria . . . they are all arrays! Kids start competing for who can notice and name the arrays first. For weeks after, kids will run up to me, breathlessly, and exclaim, "Miss. The bookshelf. It's. An. Array!"

The arrays have always been there. Children have lived among these arrays. They have used arrays to help them understand the world. Their little bodies have been organized into arrays to form lines as they walk through the school hallways. Yet until third grade, they have never formally noticed arrays. Once children have been shown examples of arrays and given the language to describe them, they start to see them everywhere.

This is what it is like to see the culture of power. It has always been there, informing and dictating our lives, but so many of us live inside it without ever recognizing it exists. In order to empower children, we need to understand how a culture of power plays out in classrooms. As education reform leader Dr. Lisa Delpit explains, the culture of power is deeply ingrained in learning. "The power of the teacher over the students; the power of the publishers of textbooks and the developers of the curriculum to determine the view of the world presented; the power of the state in enforcing compulsory schooling; and the power of the individual or group to determine another's intelligence or 'normalcy.'" The layers of power are so deep they are difficult to fully recognize.

Seth Kreisberg, author of *Transforming Power: Domination, Empowerment, and Education*, says, "Schools are places in which relationships of dominations are played out extensively every day between teachers and students, and always this domination is justified as [being] in the best interests of students." We don't want to think of our schools or recreation centers or homes as places of domination and control. As adults, we don't want to think that we possess authoritarian traits. But in order to empower others, we must see what is truly there. Every inch of our schools, our classrooms, and our neighborhoods are covered in issues of power and control.

A fence is power and control. Most of my students live in a cluster of three-story brick apartment buildings. Hundreds of children live within just four blocks. There isn't much outside space for children, but there is a grassy courtyard ringed by apartment buildings. However, that particular green grass is surrounded by an imposing wooden plank fence. Some fences direct traffic, some fences keep dangerous equipment guarded, and some fences keep out intruders. That fence was put there so children would not chase each other around or do cartwheels on that gorgeous grass. If children did play on the grass in front of their homes, presumably, the grass might be trampled on. It might get patchy. That wouldn't look nice. So there is a fence.

Roads are also power and control. If you look on a map of the apartments that most of my students live in, you will see something interesting. The western boundary of the city of Denver is mostly made up of a straight, four-lane thoroughfare, Sheridan Boulevard. Curiously, the city boundaries jut out abruptly to exactly circle the apartment buildings and a few blocks of houses where most of my students live. Instead of being a part of the more affluent county that surrounds the apartments on three sides and the multimillion dollar homes just 2,136 feet away from that fenced-in grass courtyard, the apartments are part of Denver proper. While the school district does provide buses to pick up kids in the morning and drop off kids in the afternoon, the location of these apartments means that in order for children to walk to their school or library or recreation center, even the nearest park in their own city, they must first cross one of the busiest streets in Denver.

What communities choose to emphasize and invest in demonstrates power and control, too. Michael Bonner, a second-grade teacher, recounts a story from his hometown of Perquimans County, North Carolina, in his book, *Get Up or Give Up*. While Perquimans is a small community, it is well known for the athleticism of its young people. When Michael was young, the town decided to build both a basketball court and a tennis court for the residents to enjoy. The children of Perquimans were excited by the newness of the projects. They were thrilled to finally play on a real concrete basketball court, even if it didn't have painted lines and closed at sundown because there was no lighting. However, when the tennis court was built, the facility remained open late into the night because the town invested in street lights to illuminate the area.

Interestingly, the people of Perquimans have always come together around its basketball team. Playing basketball in college and beyond has long been a dream of so many of the young residents. Few people in the town even play tennis. To this day, Perquimans County does not even have an official tennis team. Yet, it was the tennis court that got the paint and the lights. The resources did not go to where they were most needed; they went to where people in power wanted them.

Michael told me, "It is unfortunate when a community misuses power to devalue children. But it is even more of an atrocity when a child feels helpless in their own school and community. As an educator, I still distinctly remember heart-wrenching conversations with friends and students who expressed how they felt powerless and did not feel valued as human beings."

Courtyards, roads, basketball courts—most adults navigate through these spaces without noticing the complex network of power and control. Interestingly, being relatively oblivious to these components of our culture is a luxury that only the powerful enjoy. Dr. Delpit explains, "Those with power are frequently least aware of—or least willing to acknowledge—its existence. Those with less power are often most aware of its existence." We adults have a common blind spot when it comes to power, precisely because we have it. Adults see those fences simply as fences, children see those fences for what they are—barriers.

Once we are aware of the structures of power and control, we can evaluate them, challenge them, and even change them when needed. What's more, we can teach children to do the same. By naming the structures of power in a child's world, we can help young people understand their place among them.

Spark the Conversation

- What does it mean to have power?

- Is power good or bad?

- Is there a part of your life where you feel empowered?

- What are you in charge of? What am I in charge of? Should that ever change?

Understanding a young person's initial impression of power can help direct the conversation. When a young person believes power is bad, it is usually because they have experienced power in an oppressive way. They might be hesitant to describe themselves as powerful because they don't want to be seen as controlling. If this happens, help that young person see that power isn't just domination; power can be based in relationships. People can join together to make their communities stronger. Young people can join in and eventually become leaders.

Another way to begin talking about power is to examine where the young person feels a sense of control. Maybe they feel empowered on their volleyball team, in their band, or in their religious community. This can be a good way to discuss what empowerment feels like.

There is also an opportunity for us as caring adults to reflect on how we are sharing our power with the young people in our lives. Perhaps that young person can help you see an area where you can relinquish control.

2

Young Agents for Change

Childish.

What comes to minds when you hear that word? My guess is the word childish brings to mind actions and beliefs that are immature, demanding, and selfish. Is this meaning what we should associate with a word that is defined as "like a child"? Adora Svitak, just twelve years old at the time, made this point during her 2010 TED Talk: "We should abolish this age-discriminatory word, when it comes to criticizing behavior associated with irresponsibility and irrational thinking."

She is right. Framing the very characteristics of childhood in a negative light creates an environment where children are not lifted up to meet challenges. As Svitak says, "When expectations are low, trust me, we will sink to them."

We adults need to elevate and even revere the very nature of childhood. We need to name the amazing qualities that make children such effective agents of change. The good news is there are so, so many.

Adaptability

I am always amazed by the ability of children to navigate social grouping. Student mobility impacts my classroom. In 2018, 20 percent of my students joined my classroom in the middle of the school year. Walking into an established learning or working environment is understandably intimidating, even for adults. Think of all the adults you know who avoid new social situations. I have a friend who turned down a job opportunity because she "doesn't know anyone there."

Yet, several times a year a new eight-year-old walks right into my classroom. They enter into a new school, a new set of rules and expectations, and a new group of peers, and they get down to the business of learning with remarkable ease. Of course there are always children with complicated circumstances, but the majority of new kids seem like old friends in a matter of days.

Then there are the daily lives of middle school and high school students, which are ruled by bells and class schedules. Each day students are required to physically move to a different location, work with a different combination of peers, use different intellectual skills, and learn a different academic content every hour or so. Kids must be artistic at 8 a.m., mathematical at 9 a.m., learn a new language at 10 a.m., and to top it off, climb a rope in front of their peers in the gymnasium at 11 a.m.

Think about that. Think of the social skills and personal fortitude required to adapt to each new school day. Be honest, if that routine were laid out in a job description, most adults would not even apply. Yet preteens do this every day, 180 days a year, all while their own bodies are playing a Ping-Pong game with hormones. This is a shining example of adaptability. It's amazing. It's admirable. And it's rarely celebrated.

Maybe if we called this out for kids, if we held up their daily versatility, children would retain their adaptability as they grow up.

Try this . . .
OPPORTUNITY LIST

Research shows us that adaptability is crucial. After a study of nearly one thousand Australian high school students, Dr. Andrew Martin, a research fellow at the University of Sydney, found that "Young people who are more adaptable were more likely to participate in class, enjoy school, be more satisfied with life, have higher self-esteem, and have a more concrete sense of meaning and purpose in life." It's clear that if we want young people to feel like

(Continues)

(TRY THIS: Opportunity List, Cont.)

confident participants in their community, they need to be adaptable. While some kids seem to inherently display this skill, others struggle. It's important to remember that, as with all skills, adaptability can be learned.

One strategy suggested by Dr. Martin is to list the opportunities a new or uncertain situation can provide. It can look like this:

OPPORTUNITIES OF MOVING TO A NEW APARTMENT

1. Reorganize my things

2. Meet new neighbors

3. Explore a different part of my town

4. Start fresh at a new school

OPPORTUNITIES OF PRESENTING MY BOOK REPORT

1. Introduce my classmates to a book I enjoyed

2. Practice speaking clearly in front of a group

3. Share something new I learned

4. Prove that I can do something that makes me nervous

Emotional Vulnerability

Vulnerability is another resource possessed by children, which adults take for granted. Some adults believe that vulnerability is a negative trait, that a vulnerable person is somehow weak or needy. In my experience, children do not always share this attitude about being emotionally open. Instead, students in my school have shown incredible vulnerability and have reaped the rewards of being supported by their peers.

Every school year, I launch my classroom community with an activity I learned as a student teacher called "Me Bags." I start by showing the class my own Me Bag. It is a plain paper bag that holds a pair of plastic glasses shaped like cat eyes, to show I love cats. There is a *catrina maestra*—a skeleton figurine of a teacher my sister brought me from Oaxaca, Mexico. I also have two photographs of my grandmothers, one of which has passed away. When I show these items, I tell a little story and explain why each object is important to me. It is an opportunity for my students to get to know me not just as their teacher, but also as a person.

Then it's their turn. I give all the kids a paper bag and tell them to fill the bag with items that are special to them. They can bring anything they would like, although I did once have to clarify bringing your pet rat to school in your Me Bag was not an option. For the next week or so, the bags come streaming in. Kids stand at the front of the class and share a little bit about their lives. They often bring in a lot of little toys from kids' meals, medals they won in tournaments, or their favorite books.

It might sound surprising to others, but after all these years I have come to expect that kids don't just scratch the surface. They openly share intimate parts of their lives with their peers. Kids have brought in special drawings a loved one sent from prison, pictures of a parent who has passed away, a postcard from a family member who was deported, or a special stuffed animal a police officer gave them during a very scary night. When given the opportunity to share something or hide something, most children choose to share. Many children desperately want to be known and are willing to disclose details of their lives that most adults are reluctant to. The ease at which my students are able to open themselves up emotionally is admirable.

Never once have I heard or seen any of my students violate this vulnerability. They do not tease or joke. They allow their classmate to share and be heard. It is an opportunity to emotionally connect with each other, and these little bags set the tone for the rest of the year.

Every morning, I use a strategy called "Celebration, Question, or Concern," where I invite students to share one of the three options. Kids share exciting moments most of the time, but sometimes they share something they are struggling with, like the loss of a loved one. Obviously, if a child shares something that requires me to seek more intensive support, I do, but I also model how a supportive friend reacts to someone's emotional openness. I say something like, "That sounds pretty heavy. Is it something you think about a lot?" or "It must be difficult to be away from your loved ones. Is that true?" I teach my students to do the same and have even made simple posters in my room that list "Ways to Comfort Others" with options such as asking someone how they feel, listening to their story, telling them you care, or saying I'm sorry that happened. We may not be able to fix their problem or take away their pain, but we will be there for them. I want each child to know they have a whole classroom of friends who are ready and willing to help them through challenging and vulnerable times. And I want each child to know how to become that supportive friend.

Vulnerability is a resource. If a young person wants to see a change in their community, they will have to connect with others on an emotional level. They will have to share how an unfair policy affects them, how difficult it is to be denied opportunities, or how they feel when resources are not shared equitably. It is personal connections that compel us to change the status quo. We can help young people draw on their natural ability to be emotionally vulnerable so they can make a difference in their communities.

We can teach children there is power and strength in vulnerability.

> I wish that people and kids will be nice and get treated equally.

Empathy

One year, all the third-grade classes read the novel *Long Walk to Water* by Linda Sue Park. It weaves together the true story of eleven-year-old Salva Dut's heroic journey to find safety during the Second Sudanese Civil War and the story of a fictional girl, Nya, who must walk hours a day to access clean water. By the end of the book, the reader realizes that the real Salva Dut has survived and returned to drill fresh water wells in his homeland, including Nya's village.

The story is gorgeous, suspenseful, and inspiring. We decided as a class to help Salva Dut on his mission to provide clean water. The kids made crafts and sold lemonade. For each dollar raised, the kids agreed to walk one lap around our school track. At the end of our campaign, I was surprised to find that we had raised $299.16. We marched all the third-graders outside so each kid could do their share of the 299 laps.

Everything was going according to plan until we neared the end. I noticed Alicia, an enthusiastic child with a head full of wavy hair, had stopped walking and had sat down in the grass. I figured she was just taking a break, but as I looked closer, I noticed Alicia was taking off her shoes and socks. "Alicia!" I hollered, "What are you doing?"

Completely unphased, she responded, "I'm taking off my shoes."

"Why?" I shouted back.

"Oh, you know the girl in the story, Nya," Alicia explained, "She didn't have shoes when she walked to get water, so I'm going to feel what she felt. That's empathy, Miss."

As Alicia walked around the track without her shoes or socks, the other kids asked her what she was doing. She explained to them just what she had told me, and something even more surprising happened. The kids she talked to took off their shoes and socks as well. More and more kids took off their socks and shoes until, soon, the entire group of third-graders was completely barefoot.

The other teachers and I took in this scene. It was quite the sight to behold. The track at our school is not a cushioned, rubber athletic track. It is not even a paved concrete track. Our track is made up of dirt with jagged gravel scattered on top. Yet every single child chose to hobble awkwardly, as little pieces of stone dug into their bare feet. One little boy had sprained his ankle earlier in the week and was wearing a brace. He hopped the entire track on one shoeless foot.

I was blown away by the spontaneous compassion of these kids. Yes, we had talked about understanding others perspectives, and I knew my students could explain the concept of empathy, but I did not realize just how deeply, how naturally, they internalized what it means to be empathetic. That empathy is powerful.

There are many other examples of young people being empowered to make a difference through their compassion for others, like Jessie Rees who was eleven years old when she was diagnosed with a brain tumor. Every day, Jessie and her family would drive to the hospital for treatment. She noticed that while she went home every night to her family and her own bed, many of her fellow patients did not. They stayed at the hospital every day and every night.

Jessie came up with the idea of Joy Jars. She found old jars in her kitchen and filled them with toys, stickers, and crayons. She passed out the jars to kids at the hospital. "I just wanted to make them happier because I know they are going through a lot, too," Jessie explained in an interview.

Jessie was able to make and give away three thousand Joy Jars before she passed away, but the legacy of her empathy lives on. Her family has continued her work through their website Jessie. org and their foundation. To date they have filled and distributed two hundred thousand Joy Jars to kids fighting cancer in all fifty states and forty countries.

Even very young children can blow you away with their empathy. Four-year-old Austin Perine was watching a TV show about pandas. The mother panda abandoned the baby panda. Austin's father explained the situation to his son by saying the baby panda was now homeless. Austin asked an innocent and poignant question, "Dad, are people homeless?"

From that day on Austin asked his mother and father if he could spend all of his allowance and the money they would spend on toys on food for the homeless instead. Now, once a week donning his signature blue shirt and red cape, Austin passes out chicken sandwiches and drinks to people who are homeless in his hometown of Birmingham, Alabama.

He says his superhero name is President Austin because, as his dad explained, helping people is Austin's idea of what a president is supposed to do. When asked by a reporter why he does this, Austin replied, "You know what, Mr. Steve, it's just the right thing to do."

Alicia, Jessie, and Austin teach us just how powerful the empathy of young people can be. Adults can and should expect tremendous levels of insight and compassion from children.

I wish that we would feed and provide shelter for the poor. This will help the poor have a happy and better life. This will also keep them from getting sick and give them a place to sleep. If you were poor you would want someone to give you water, food, and shelter. We should all work as a community to take care of our poor and keep them safe.

MY WISH FOR THE WORLD

Angela Cobián, elected director, Denver Board of Education

Adults who work with students should know that empowerment is a process. It is not a one-way transferal of knowledge or power from teacher to student. Empowerment is about creating spaces, experiences, and opportunities for young people to realize they are already powerful.

I learned this lesson as a ninth-grade student when my high school Honors English teacher, Ms. Bristow, was relentless in her encouragement. She kept pushing me to attend a speech and debate tournament. After repeatedly turning her invitations down, Ms. Bristow told me, "You are smart, passionate, and aggressive. You have a lot to say, and people need to hear it." Ms. Bristow was not just inviting me to join a club; rather, she clearly named the potential she saw in my powerful fifteen-year-old self and extended an opportunity to refine and apply my skills in high school forensics.

I had never heard about the world of high school speech and debate because it included elite public and private schools. The forensics circuit had both explicit and implicit norms around culture and dress that were completely foreign. No one ever told me to wear a suit—the most obvious of forensics' social norms. The students from one nearby elite public high school snickered when I walked up to the front of

(Continues)

(MY WISH FOR THE WORLD, Angela Cobián, Cont.)

the room in a corduroy mini skirt and knee high socks to give my first speech. At first I felt embarrassed at my ignorance. Fortunately, moxie outweighed shame as I remembered my teacher's confidence in my ability. Suit or no suit, I had tenaciously researched and prepared a pro and con speech for every debate topic that day. As such, I kept giving speeches, getting better each time I spoke.

Growing up the daughter of Mexican immigrants, learning a second language, transiently attending many elementary schools had formed me into an adaptable, insatiably curious, and resilient teenager. These skills had led me to over-prepare for my first speech and debate tournament. Combined with my confidence, I was awarded the second-place prize of "Superior Speaker" that day. I ended up participating in speech and debate through my junior year of college which, in hindsight, prepared me to give stump speeches on the campaign trail and debate my opponent in my recent campaign and subsequent election to represent my community on the Denver Board of Education.

To be clear, encouraging youth occasionally is not enough. In my case, there was a sustained and concerted effort by many adults. Before Ms. Bristow, my middle school principal Mr. Fore was the first to ask me what I wanted to achieve with my life and leadership. Most importantly, my parents were always there to take pictures of my ribbons and trophies and explain that in their eyes, I could do anything. Indeed, a community organizing principle states: *the first revolution is internal.*

I benefited from so many adults who recognized my inveterate power. They opened the door of opportunity and let me walk through it; *this* is empowerment.

I wish youth, especially those from underrepresented communities, realize their experiences uniquely qualify them to be the leaders our country needs and deserves.

Anger

Anger isn't often considered a resource, but it should be. Anger is a strong emotional reaction to perceived provocation or wrongdoing. Injustice, inequity, unfairness all justifiably provoke anger. Young people can use that anger and frustration to drive change.

"I had been following the Flint, Michigan, issue for about two years," eleven-year-old Gitanjali Rao told *ABC News*. "I was appalled by the number of people affected by lead contamination in water."

Gitanjali knew that Flint was the most infamous case of lead contamination of the water supply, but it was far from the only one. Later, she read an article on an MIT website. It explained a new technology that could be used to detect hazardous substances in the air. She thought perhaps it could be used to determine if lead was present in water. She invented a device called TETHYS, named after the Greek god of fresh water. The device uses carbon nanotube sensors connected to a custom app, which Gitanjali also created. In a matter of seconds, the device can detect lead in water faster and cheaper than other current methods.

Gitanjali is clearly an impressive young scientist, but she was motivated to innovate by her strong reaction to the Flint water crisis. That frustration was an asset.

Sunrose Guerrero also used anger to motivate her work. As a young Indigenous woman, she waited year after year for her culture to be taught or even mentioned in school. In high school, her history teacher asked the class to make a list of events considered tragedies by historians. Students listed off events such as the Holocaust, 9/11, and a local shooting, as her teacher recorded them on the whiteboard. Though Sunrose was typically shy in class, that day she decided to raise her hand. She offered the example of the Massacre at Wounded Knee where hundreds of unarmed Lakota men, women, and children were killed by U.S. cavalry troops in 1890. For reasons still unclear to Sunrose, her teacher told her this was not an acceptable example to speak about at school. When Sunrose insisted the massacre be listed, she was told to leave the classroom.

"I was usually a very calm person, but at that moment I felt so much anger," Sunrose told me. "I was angry that my culture and the history of my people were rarely seen as valuable enough to be taught in school. When it was taught, it was full of inaccuracies and mischaracterizations. I just couldn't stay silent anymore."

Sunrose started interviewing friends and found that she was not alone. So many of her classmates felt as though their cultures were not included in the curriculum either. This led Sunrose to help organize a conference for Native and Indigenous youth in her community. She then became the Native student representative in her school district and even presented her recommendations to the state board of education. She continues to advocate for accurate textbooks, offering courses that teach the history and culture of Indigenous people, and for schools to remove antiquated stereotypes harmful to Indigenous people.

"Yeah, I'm angry, but my work doesn't come from a place of anger," Sunrose explains. "It comes from a place of compassion. I want everyone to feel honored and respected by the education system." Sunrose's anger doesn't consume her; it empowers her.

Dr. Dena Simmons, assistant director of the Yale Center for Emotional Intelligence, also sees this empowerment in her work. She has found that many adults hold the misconception that anger is uncontrollable and leads exclusively to negative outcomes. In reality, "We can transform our anger into activism, especially if we consider the genesis of anger," says Dr. Simmons. Anger is related to being wronged in some way. "The key to making anger useful is to use emotional regulation strategies that lead to productive outcomes instead of letting anger derail us," says Dr. Simmons. She recommends teaching young people simple strategies like breathing deeply, visualizing a more just outcome, and creating a plan for changing the situation.

When a young person feels anger, disappointment, or frustration about a situation in their life, don't ignore it. Explore it. Find out more about the cause of such a strong reaction. Likely it is an emotional response to unfairness or injustice. If we step in and help a young person see what actions can be taken, their anger can be the catalyst for change.

The casual observer might think that young people are more interested in themselves than others. But ask anyone who has cared for or taught children, and they can give you numerous examples of just how big hearted children can truly be. This book is filled with those instances, and, trust me, there are so many more examples I could include.

Vivian Gussin Paley, teacher and researcher, calls attention to this impulsive goodness in her book, *The Kindness of Children*. She describes this so eloquently when she says, "I've been watching young children most of my life, and they are more often kind to each other than unkind. The early instinct to help someone is powerful."

Adaptability, vulnerability, empathy, and even anger—these are the qualities that should come to mind when we use the world childish. They are each a gift of childhood. The more we adults ignore these gifts and demand our own versions of perfection, the more these qualities fade. We can leverage children's inherent kindness and creativity to help children discover themselves and their place in the world. We can help children stand up for themselves and what they believe in. That starts when we honor the unique qualities of childhood.

Spark the Conversation

- What qualities make you uniquely qualified to make a difference in the world?

- Tell me about a time when you were vulnerable.

- How can empathy be powerful?

- What makes you angry? What can you do about it?

Young people do not need to wait until they grow up to start making a difference in their community. They have so many wonderful traits and attributes that will help them work toward a goal right now. Help them see this. A child may not see a quality like empathy or vulnerability as powerful, but it is.

A great way to start is by finding examples in their own life where they have made a difference in some small way. Maybe they asked a classmate without many friends to sit with them at lunch. That shows that they have the ability to notice when someone is left out and make an effort to include them. Maybe they pushed back when someone made a biased statement, that means they can stand up for what is right. These small moments can build to something bigger.

I wish...If my teachers
would notice all
the kids that are
alone and get bullird.
Kids who want a
friend.

3

It Starts with Belonging

Our school has a special feature on our playground. It is a simple green bench that sits in between the monkey bars and the baseball field. It looks like most metal benches at public parks but has the words "buddy bench" written on the backrest.

When Christian Bucks was eight years old, he talked to his principal about an idea that would "eliminate loneliness and foster friendship on the playground." All they would need was a bench and a sign. If a child needs someone to play with, they can walk over and have a seat on the buddy bench. When other children see someone sitting on the buddy bench, they know to offer to play with them. It's that simple, and it works. I was talking to a little boy, and mid-sentence he glanced over and saw another kid sit down on the buddy bench. The boy bolted over to the bench, and a couple seconds later they are both on the swings.

Just the presence of the bench sends a message. It normalizes the idea that kids feel alone sometimes. It also communicates that at our school, you won't have to feel lonely for long. There are people here who care about you. There are people who will seek you out and include you.

This is the level of belonging that all children deserve to have.

Too often kids don't get this level of support. Many kids feel like high school student Natalie Hampton. She experienced severe bullying in middle school. She felt alone and invisible. "Apart from the verbal taunts and violence," Natalie explained, "one of the worst things was having to eat lunch alone, and the embarrassment of having others see me eating lunch alone." Eventually, she changed schools and found new friends. But Natalie didn't want other kids to feel ostracized the same way she had.

Many adults bemoan the rise of social media. They see only the potential for misuse and abuse, but at fifteen years old, Natalie used the power of social platforms for good. She came up with the idea for a free app called Sit With Us. To Natalie, "The first step to a warmer, more inclusive community can begin with lunch." The app helps kids find classmates to sit with in the cafeteria. It does this by taking kids who are looking for tables and kids at tables who are willing to welcome kids and pairs them together. Once kids download the app and create a profile, they can search for tables at their school. This way, they can sit down without fear of rejection.

Often, social media gains the most attention when it is causing harm, and unfortunately that harm can be very real. Natalie herself experienced the pain of cyberbullying, and yet she found a way to use the power of social media and technology to bring people together. She had experienced the sting of isolation and chose to find a way to help others feel like they belong.

As she said in her 2017 TED Talk, "Even if you don't use the app, you can embody the spirit of Sit With Us by inviting someone alone over to your table. You never know—your future best friend might be sitting at the next table over."

Belonging Is a Need

Belonging is not like water or food. A human can survive only about one hundred hours without water and a few weeks without food. How long could a human survive without love, without acceptance, or without belonging?

It's helpful to think of a need not strictly as a physiological requirement, but rather as a central human motivation. Belonging, defined as the need to be an accepted member of part of a group, drives so much of our daily behavior, whether we are aware of it or not. This need to feel a part of a group was most famously described by Abraham Maslow in his theory of human motivation. In his hierarchy of five basic needs, Maslow places the need to feel love and belongingness only after the physiological needs like food, water, and safety.

The research of Roy Baumeister and Mark Leary has been perhaps the most influential when it comes to understanding the need for belonging. They believe that belonging is even more essential than Maslow claims. They explain, "Again and again, we found evidence of a basic desire to form social attachments. People form social bonds readily, even under seemingly adverse conditions." It is clear from their research that humans will go to great lengths to form connections with others. We are reluctant to end relationships, even when they are challenging and sometimes even when they are physically or emotionally harmful. That paradox—that humans at times will sacrifice comfort and safety to receive love and acceptance—proves just how fundamental the need to belong is.

While that might sound ominous, it is actually good news. We do not have to convince a child that belonging is a worthy pursuit precisely because all of us have an innate urge to find acceptance in a group. It's like gravity. You do not have to convince a ball to roll down a hill. You do not have to cajole it or force it. The ball will roll down the hill as long as all the obstacles have been removed.

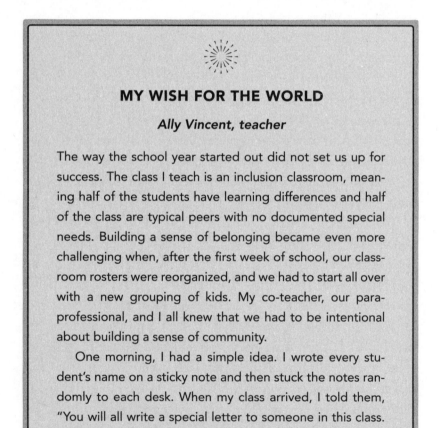

MY WISH FOR THE WORLD

Ally Vincent, teacher

The way the school year started out did not set us up for success. The class I teach is an inclusion classroom, meaning half of the students have learning differences and half of the class are typical peers with no documented special needs. Building a sense of belonging became even more challenging when, after the first week of school, our classroom rosters were reorganized, and we had to start all over with a new grouping of kids. My co-teacher, our paraprofessional, and I all knew that we had to be intentional about building a sense of community.

One morning, I had a simple idea. I wrote every student's name on a sticky note and then stuck the notes randomly to each desk. When my class arrived, I told them, "You will all write a special letter to someone in this class. Explain what you appreciate about that person and why they belong in this class. The name of the person you will write to is written on a sticky note on your desk. Go!" I was happy to see that not a single student complained or even hesitated, they just got right to work. Even students who struggled with writing showed so much determination to write a letter and deliver it to a classmate.

I remember how much this activity affected Jace. Jace was the kind of kid who was always hard on himself. He struggled with reading and writing, his frustration often turning into self-loathing. Constantly, Jace would say, "I'm stupid" and "I shouldn't be in this class."

When Jace received his first letter, he rushed right over to me and asked, "What does it say?" As I read the words from his classmate, I saw a smile roll across his face. Something was changing in him. I knew this letter writing was something I had to keep doing.

Every few weeks, usually on a Friday morning, I would lay out a new set of sticky notes. The kids would eagerly write and draw a note to a newly assigned friend. Most kids took the letters home to show their family, but Jace did something different. He kept all of the notes neatly in a blue folder. When school got tricky and Jace got down on himself, I'd tell him to take out that blue folder. I patiently told him what each letter said. I could tell with each rereading the inner voice that said "You belong here" was getting louder than the voice that said "You're not good enough."

I wish the world would allow every child to realize that they are loved and needed.

I wish everyone was treated equally, no matter their race, gender, or sexuality. I wish the world was filled with kindness. I wish we could all work together to save the Earth from pollution + climate change. I dream of helping to change the world.

Belonging Is an Exchange

As an adult, it is tempting to believe that a sense of belonging is something you provide and a child accepts. The truth is, belonging is an exchange. Baumeister and Leary state the obvious when they say, "Love is highly satisfying and desirable only if it is mutual." We don't need to provide one-way belonging, we need to provide the opportunity for mutuality, a sense of sharing and contributing to a relationship. Think of belonging not as welcoming someone into your home, but rather as building a home with others.

Children in my classroom, like every classroom in the world, are always falling down or tripping over things. It seems like once a day a student has a minor bump or bruise that sends them into tears. As a brand new teacher, I would drop everything and rush right over to help. The more I teach, the less I do that. I realized that by always swooping in to comfort a student, I was robbing a child from the opportunity to be a caring member of the classroom community. So when an injury is not serious (and it is very easy to tell) I send another student to help.

I don't just send whoever is closest; I am deliberate in choosing the helper. I usually call upon a child who struggles to fit in or make friends. Why? Because that is the kid who needs practice. That is the kid who might not take the initiative to help out but is very capable of showing kindness. Each little fall is a chance for a child who struggles relating to their peers to feel the inner satisfaction that comes from showing compassion. The trick is that helping doesn't always come naturally to this kid, so I am explicit in my instructions. I tell them exactly what they need to do to contribute. I'll say, "Go get a wet paper towel to put on her bruise and sit with her until she feels better" or "Help him stand up and get a drink of water."

Once the minor crisis is over, I follow up both with the kid who got hurt and the kid who helped. I make sure they realize that their community took care of them. I'll ask questions like, when you got hurt who was there for you? Why do you think he helped you? What does it feel like to know others will support you when you need it? I'll ask the helper, what did you do that was helpful? How did it feel? These are the type of short exchanges that help children not only feel supported, but also give children the opportunity to support each other.

Belonging is just as much about your responsibility to a group as it is about your acceptance by a group. Christopher Emdin, professor and author, advocates for assigning every child a particular responsibility in the classroom such as equipment distributor, desk arranger, even joke teller. In Emdin's class, students are held accountable for their role so no one else is allowed to do that task on their behalf. In Emdin's book, *For White Folks Who Teach in the Hood . . . and the Rest of Y'all Too*, he says,

In one case, a student was assigned the role of "eraser of the chalkboard." While it may be perceived as an insignificant role, it was clear to students that it was an important role when the student assigned to it skipped class one day. That day, there were notes that I wanted to write and that students needed to copy. However, because the eraser of the chalkboard did not come to school that day, the board did not get erased. While other students volunteered to complete the task, I ensured that no one did. The fallout from the students' failure to perform his assigned role results in healthy peer pressure from the class in holding him accountable for the disruption.

The "eraser of the board" was needed by the class. It was that student's responsibility that cemented belonging.

In my own classroom, I have seen clearly defined roles hold a great deal of importance for my students. They take pride in being the person who answers the phone or holds open the door. One year, one of my students asked earnestly if he could be the official riddle master and challenged the class to solve weekly riddles. These roles are a small way of allowing young people to feel like they belong, by giving them opportunities to contribute. Get kids involved. Remember that belonging is not one-sided; it is an exchange.

The Power of Friendship

I have learned to leverage friendships between students in my classroom. In my first years of teaching, I considered friendships a distraction to learning. I thought if I allowed friends to sit together they would just mess around. Over the years, I have realized how wrong I was. Now I know if I set firm expectations for behavior and provide sufficient supports, kids who are friends are able to focus, complete assignments, and learn with each other. In fact, friendships make my students happier and more confident. Friendship can be a safety blanket in the best sense of the word.

I have seen powerful friendships develop between kids who on the surface may seem very different. My school uses the inclusion model. This means that students who have significant special needs spend part of their day in smaller classes designed to meet their particular needs and part of the day in classrooms, like mine, with their typical peers.

I have heard some debate from non-educators about this being a distraction in the classroom, or students with special needs not being able to fit in with others. Simply put, this is just not what I have experienced. On the contrary, inclusion has added significantly to the sense of belonging in our classroom.

It is a true exchange. Students with special needs might be limited physically or have developmental delays, but they are perfectly able not only to participate but also to contribute to the classroom community. My students are able to connect with someone who has a different perspective on the world. I have seen so many of my students blossom by being a supportive peer to a student with special needs. The way they naturally respond with patience and care is powerful. One day out of the corner of my eye, I saw a couple students flailing round in the back of the classroom. When I looked closer I realized that one of my students was teaching a student who was nonverbal how to dab. The friendships formed between my students and students with disabilities foster a lifelong value for diversity and an understanding of the dignity of every human being. Kids realize that we are all more alike than we are different.

MY WISH FOR THE WORLD

Joe "Mr. D" Dombrowski, teacher,
comedian, social media content creator

It was a completely unremarkable day of third grade. The only reason I remember that day at all was because it was the first time I heard that word. A boy had said to another kid, "You're gay!"

"What's that?" I asked.

Matter of factly, he explained, "Gay is when you are a boy, but you act like a girl."

My first reaction was relief. My entire life, I knew I was different. I just knew in my heart, in my body, in the way I reacted to the world. I was different. I was weird. I didn't fully belong. I could never put a word to that experience, but the feeling was always present. Maybe "gay" was the name for it.

"Oh, I think I'm gay," I thought. I somehow knew it was something I could not say aloud. I soon learned that in my world, gay was not a description—it was an accusation. I immediately received the message that gay people didn't belong in my community.

Until middle school, I legitimately thought I was the only gay person in the entire world. The only one. That is not an exaggeration. One day, I hid in my bedroom closet—a literal one, I know—and whispered to myself slowly and deliberately, "I . . . am . . . gay." Those words were monumental, groundbreaking.

By fourteen years old, I was out, but I didn't find a true sense of belonging. I was carrying around a constant burden that I had to win everyone over. I was gay, but I could be funny. If I was funny enough, I would be liked and accepted, and then it wouldn't even matter that I was gay.

Years passed, and I went away to college. I met people who helped me remove my mask of humor and deflection. I found the welcoming community I had been looking for. That acceptance allowed me to explore my curiosities and discover my interests. I developed a love of education. I found a place, in the front of my own classroom, where I could stand in my own authenticity, a place where I belonged.

To think that there are children who feel alone in their experience—that breaks my heart and drives my work. Every child has a need to find belonging. In my classroom, I make sure every student is seen and celebrated. I know because I've seen it, when a child feels free to be themselves, there are no limits to their learning.

That's why I started the #EmbraceYourWeird campaign, first in my own classroom and then on social media. We each have something about us that the world is ready to label as weird. Weird is wonderful. When everyone embraces their individual weirdness, we create welcoming communities.

I wish that through embracing ourselves, we can embrace others.

This type of school culture is transformative. Our special education teacher, Lynn Malie, explains, "All my students have significant disabilities, which make them vulnerable to feeling isolated in school. We push back against that by highly valuing their contributions to our community. Hearing my students' names being called out in the hallways by friends from around the school is one of the most gratifying experiences of my teaching career."

One of my students put it perfectly. Our caterpillars had just transformed into butterflies, but one had emerged with bent wings and seemed like the fragile insect would not make it very long. I was about to take it out of the butterfly enclosure and dispose of it, when a student responded in horror. He said, "Miss! What are you doing? Just 'cause it's not perfect doesn't mean you should take it away!"

The same is true for people. It's a goal of mine to make sure each of my students has true friends because friendship is a key component of belonging. But that doesn't mean every student needs to be friends with every single kid in class. When it comes to friends, one or two will do. Researchers Baumeister and Leary found that "People need a few close relationships, and forming additional bonds beyond those few has less and less impact. Having two as opposed to no close relationships may make a world of difference to the person's health and happiness; having eight as opposed to six may have very little consequence." We don't have to saddle children with the burden of having to build meaningful friendships with everyone in the class or youth group or soccer team. If we want to help children and young people feel like they belong, we can start with helping them form one or two relationships.

Belonging First

Belonging is a central psychological need. When the need to belong is not met, we feel anxious and uneasy. That's why your heart beats a little faster where you walk into a room full of people you don't know. It's why you might find it difficult to speak up during a meeting when you are the new person at the office. It's also why children become reticent, stressed, and sometimes impulsive when they cannot find the acceptance they seek.

The psychological stress of not belonging distracts us from other cognitive tasks such as learning, solving problems, being creative, or feeling joy. When I asked Dr. Leary what we needed to know about belonging, he said, "Students certainly put social relations and belonging ahead of, say, learning arithmetic or social studies. So until their social needs are met, they can't fully devote themselves to less psychologically pressing concerns such as schoolwork."

Research tells us more about the impact of belonging. Dr. Carissa Romero of the Mindset Scholars Network explains, "Students who are confident they belong and are valued by their teachers and peers are able to engage more fully in learning. They have fewer behavior problems, are more open to critical feedback, take greater advantage of learning opportunities, build important relationships, and generally have more positive attitudes about their class work and teachers. In turn, they are more likely to persevere in the face of difficulty and do better in school."

We must see belonging for what it is—a fundamental human need. It drives the behavior and emotions of us all, especially children. If a child does not find a sense of belonging, they will pour all of their emotional energy into ending their own isolation.

Try this . . .

HOW TO BE A BFF

The idea of a best friend is ageless, but according to the *New Oxford American Dictionary*, the term BFF, meaning best friend forever, originated in 1996. As far as I can tell, the popularity of this term has only grown. My students plaster "BFF" on their coloring pages and their backpacks, and they talk about their BFFs constantly. There are two concepts I teach my students about best friends:

1. Best friend is a job title, not a person

2. You are allowed to have as many best friends as you want

Kids need to know that a best friend is a good friend. Someone who is mean to you and makes you feel bad about yourself is not your best friend. If you want to be a best friend, you have to act like one—be fair, patient, and compassionate.

There is a possessive quality that tends to creep into children's idea of a best friend. They believe you can have only one, which means if your BFF declares she has a new best friend, your status has been automatically eliminated. This type of thinking causes so much torment.

The students in my class are constantly making declarations of who their BFF is, and my canned response is always the same, "That's great! How many best friends are you allowed to have?" At the beginning of the year, they look at me and cautiously say, "One?" I correct them. "Nope, you are allowed to have as many BFFs as you want." By the end of the school year when I ask how many best friends they can have, my students just roll their eyes and say, "As many as you want . . . duh."

This is when we see children change themselves. They compromise their authenticity to be liked, to be accepted, to be palatable. A facade is created to fit in. This may bring momentary relief, but the burning desire to be yourself and be accepted exactly as you are can not be extinguished. Brené Brown puts it so perfectly in her book *Braving the Wilderness*, "True belonging doesn't require you to change who you are; it requires you to be who you are."

Only when a child is accepted and valued are they are free. Free to try new things and take risks. Free to explore their curiosities and question the world around them. Free to develop their own unique identity and discover their place in the world. Free to form convictions and stand up for what they believe in. Only when a child finds belonging can they also find their own power. We all need belonging first and everything else second.

Spark the Conversation

- How do you know when you belong?

- How can you help others feel like they belong?

- How do you contribute to your community?

How do adults know if we have effectively created the conditions for belonging? Ask! Young people are very much aware of when they feel welcomed and accepted versus when they feel isolated and ostracized. Only when we know how children experience acceptance, or the lack thereof, can we respond.

Young people can also help us solve problems related to belonging. Even if a young person feels perfectly accepted and supported they can probably identify members of the class, team, or club who don't feel similarly.

A young child might notice a classmate isn't spoken to at lunch. An older child might notice it is hard for students who are still learning English to interact with their peers. Perhaps a young person notices racial tension in the community. All of these observations can lead to a greater discussion about belonging and how we all, as active members of the community, can help others feel included.

It can also be helpful to share our own experiences with belonging. As adults we have already navigated our way through countless groups and the social dynamics that come with them. We can offer a listening ear and share our wisdom.

4

The Foundations of Fairness

> I wish...that everyone gets treated corectly and that people people good theat other picked these becaise: you need to be treated verry nicely I be treate

If you have ever encountered a child emphatically refusing to share a toy or a sneaky child hoarding all the Halloween candy for themselves, you might be tempted to believe that children have an inclination to be greedy or selfish.

But research shows that children actually develop a sense of fairness that leans toward sharing equitably. A study reported in *Scientific American* found that children notice when objects are shared equally. Children are willing to punish those who have been unfair. In experiments, older children "would rather receive nothing than receive more than a peer."

Adults often issue well-meaning directives such as "share with others" and "be fair," but we sometimes fail to explain these ideas to children with any level of complexity. In my experience, children develop a nuanced understanding of fairness, with a simple nudge from an adult.

I have even seen these attitudes of fairness evolve within a sixty-minute lesson. One school year, I started the lesson by asking my students, "What does 'fair' mean?" Then I gave two options:

1. Fairness means getting what I want and everyone getting the same thing.

OR

2. Fairness means getting what you need and everyone getting the same chance.

Then we made a simple bar graph on the board. Not surprisingly, three-quarters of the class chose option one. I didn't correct them or inject my own option. Instead, I led them through a series of thought experiments.

1. My family orders pizza. My mom gets three slices of pizza, I get two slices of pizza, my little brother gets one slice of pizza.

2. Ms. Schwartz brings in candy. She gives all the boys two pieces of candy and all the girls one piece of candy.

3. The whole class has a party. At the end of the party everyone helps clean up.

After each scenario, we discussed whether or not the kids thought the situation was fair. We talked about who in the situation got what they wanted and whether or not everyone got the same thing. Watching children think critically about the concept of fairness is incredible.

Up until this point my students had spent their lives saying, "That's not fair!" whenever someone else got the toy or book they wanted. Simply asking, "If fairness is everyone getting the same thing, then should adults get the same amount of pizza as a baby brother?" and "When is it unfair for you to get more?" and "If you don't want to clean up, when is it still fair that you have to?" helps children to form a definition of fairness. At the end of the lesson, I polled the class again. Almost all students reported they now thought fairness was "everyone getting what they need and the same chance."

Questions of fairness, sharing, and equity come up every single day in my classroom. Creating a shared understanding around what fairness is has helped my students to examine their perceptions and empathize with the needs of others. My students don't resent a classmate who might get more of my attention during a math lesson and don't resent the student who gets to be the first person in line everyday. Rather, they understand that everyone had different skills and needs. And they also realize something more central.

My students realize their individual needs can be different than others, even those who seem or who are similar to them. They also learn that it's fair to have their needs addressed. And when their needs are not met, they understand it's okay to stand up for themselves. Most importantly, my students learn that when the needs of others are not met, they can advocate for others, too.

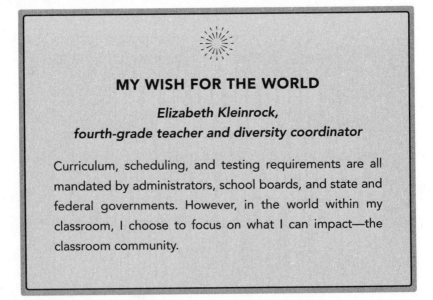

I wish... people can stop bullying other people. Because then they don't make them feel welcome. And they make them feel lonely.

MY WISH FOR THE WORLD

Elizabeth Kleinrock,
fourth-grade teacher and diversity coordinator

Curriculum, scheduling, and testing requirements are all mandated by administrators, school boards, and state and federal governments. However, in the world within my classroom, I choose to focus on what I can impact—the classroom community.

For the first two weeks of school, my top priority is always creating a sense of connectedness among my students. My former principal told me, "There is always time to re-teach a concept or re-do a lesson. You do not have a second chance to build community. Community is the one thing we cannot afford to get wrong the first time."

My students are incredibly diverse. About half of my students hail from affluent families and half qualify for free or reduced lunch. About half identify as BIPOC (Black, Indigenous, or people of color) and half identify as white. Some might see this demographic makeup as a challenge. I see it as our strength, but I know we need to create a supportive environment if I want each and every student to feel empowered. That starts with two guiding principles: respect and trust. It is as true for children as it is for adults, we can relate all interactions, positive or negative, back to presence or lack of trust and respect. Without trust and respect, there is no community. There is no collaboration, and there is no positive learning environment.

On the first day of school, I hang two blank posters on the board. In giant black letters I write the words TRUST and RESPECT. Then I ask students to write their definitions of what these words mean, and we come together to discuss our understandings. For many students, it is difficult to explain these concepts without using the words in the definitions, so we often come up with examples of what trust and respect look like, sound like, and feel like, in order to make their abstract meanings more concrete.

(Continues)

(MY WISH FOR THE WORLD, Elizabeth Kleinrock Cont.)

Trust and respect are pillars in my classroom. Most importantly, my students know these are values that also apply to me as their teacher, and they have the right to hold me accountable, which is only fair. On the first day of school, I love to read *Thank You Mr. Falker* by Patricia Polacco to my students. Following our read aloud, we discuss the qualities the students desire in their teacher. After brainstorming as a group, my students collaborate to write a "teacher contract," which I sign and display on the wall for the entire year. This activity is the foundation of building trust and respect in a classroom because it lets my students know I work for them, and they have a voice in demanding a high-quality education.

When children respect their peers, they can communicate empathetically. When children can trust their teachers, they can share their truths, passions, and curiosities.

I wish the world would make space for the voices and experiences of all children.

I wish in this world there were no homeless so no one has to suffer and everyone can have a happy life.

Consequences and Punishment

Classrooms these days are very different from when I went to school. I remember doing a lot of worksheets and being assigned books to read. Now, most elementary school classrooms have their own mini libraries where kids are able to select and read the books they are drawn to. My classroom is no different. I take a lot of pride in my classroom library. I am always on the prowl for books at thrift stores and garage sales. I get a ton of books from mini grants on a donation website called DonorsChoose.org. I try to have the most exciting, popular, culturally relevant books I can while providing children a gorgeous, well-organized library that sparks a love of reading. There is one obstacle in the way of this goal—the children themselves. Within days, those beautiful bookshelves will look like a disaster zone if kids are not taught to take responsibility for the classroom library.

On the first day of every school year, I write "Coming soon!" on a few pieces of paper and tape them up on my bookshelves. Kids are not able to read the books because they don't know the rules of the library yet. The trick is, I don't know the rules yet either. That's because every year my students create the rules of the library themselves. I lead kids through a lesson where they brainstorm and decide on rules about how many books they can have at one time, how to take care of the books so they don't rip, how to organize the books, and how long each kid can spend "book shopping." Once we have all agreed upon some pretty basic rules, I get down to my favorite part of the lesson—figuring out the consequences.

I ask kids, "What should happen if one of our friends breaks the rules? What should the consequence be?" You might expect kids would go easy on the consequences, since kids hate to be punished. You would be wrong. Every single time I have taught this lesson, kids come up with the most extreme ideas. They say things like, take away recess for a week, never get to use the library again, and go to the principal's office. One year, a little girl whose parents were both police officers proposed that the consequence for breaking the library rules should be that the child was arrested.

These ideas help me open up a much needed dialogue about consequences. The term consequence, like power, often has a negative connotation. It is especially easy for children to convolute the meaning of the word consequences with the meaning of the word punishment. Young people often think a consequence is a bad thing that happens when someone gets in trouble. The truth is, a consequence is just an outcome. We may make choices that can have positive consequences or negative consequences, but consequence itself is neutral.

I also get a chance to talk to children about punishment. The answers I get from my student to the question, "Why do kids get punished?" are always very revealing. They say things like, "Kids are punished because they break things," "Kids are punished because they talk back," or even "Kids are punished because they make someone mad." It is easy to see how, as adults, our attitudes toward consequences are reflected in these responses. These answers reveal a flawed but understandable childhood logic: consequences are punishment, and punishments are penalties for being bad.

I understand why children come to this conclusion. So often adults focus on punitive responses to wrongdoing. They think punishment will be a deterrent for future mistakes. The more severe the punishment, the more likely the misdeed will not occur again. The Center for Responsive Schools describes it this way:

The goal of punishment is to enforce compliance with the rules by using external controls or authoritarian discipline. While effective in stopping the misbehavior of the moment, punishment does little to increase student responsibility. Punishment often leads to feelings of anger, discouragement and resentment, and an increase in evasion and deception.

Punishment for the sake of discipline is just not effective. It does not change future behavior, and it certainly doesn't empower students.

I have an opportunity to help children develop a better understanding of the consequences of their choices. My approach to wrongdoing is restorative rather than punitive. The core idea is to restore the community, to repair the harm, and to make it right, not to force a child into submission.

When something goes wrong, I want kids to shift their thinking from "I am bad. I am in trouble" to a more empowering thinking that sounds like, "My choices have consequences for myself and others. When I make a mistake, I can make it right."

In the case of our classroom library, if you hurt our community by ripping up books when you got mad, you need to make it right by taping up the books. If you dump all your books on the floor, then you can make it right by organizing the books while the rest of the class engages in a fun activity. If you spend time messing around instead of reading, maybe you can make a presentation to the class on strategies that readers can use to focus when bored or distracted.

The good news is, this logical approach to consequences is actually more effective. The Center for Responsive Schools explains, "Unlike punishment, where the intention is to make a child feel shamed, the intention of logical consequences is to help children develop internal controls and to learn from their mistakes in a supportive atmosphere."

I used this logical consequence approach when I took my students on a field trip to a local nature preserve, Bluff Lake. We hiked and conducted a prairie dog census. Students counted prairie dog burrows and made observations. Across a field I caught a glimpse of one little boy walking over to a massive ant hill, and in one swift jump he planted both of his feet into the center of the ant mound. After all those lessons about ecosystems and many, many reminders to be careful of the environment, the boy had just destroyed the shelter of a colony of ants . . . in a nature preserve, no less!

At the beginning of my teaching career, I probably would have made the boy sit out for part of the hike or maybe write an apology letter when we got back to school, but over time I've realized this approach doesn't solve anything. Instead, I walked over and asked, "Do you happen to know how these footprints got on this ant hill?" He looked down. I could see that he was realizing the effect of his impulsive decision. I said, "It may have felt cool to feel the dirt squish under your feet, but now the ants don't have a home. How can we make this right?" He couldn't rebuild the ant hill, but we decided that he could make it right by helping other kids to avoid making the same mistake. The boy had a conversation with our nature guide about the prairie ecosystem, and then he presented to the class three reasons why ants are important to the food web. In this case, the boy realized he made a mistake, understood the consequences of his decision, then shared his learning with his peers. It was so much more empowering than a time out.

My hope is that by solving problems over and over again using a logical consequences approach, the impact will spread beyond my classroom. I hope it sets up a lifetime of finding resolutions to conflicts with a restorative mindset.

A great example of this is seven-year-old Cameron Thompson. He made a bad choice on the playground one day. When another little boy brought a doll to school for show and tell, Cameron gathered his friends and together they made fun of the boy until a school staff member stepped in. At home, Cameron's mom had him imagine what it would be like to be in the shoes of the other little boy. That's when Cameron had an idea to make it right.

"I felt bad about how I had treated the boy I picked on," he explained, "so I asked our principal if I could start a club to help others learn about bullying and how it makes others feel." After getting the approval of his principal, Cameron knew he would need help starting his new club. So he asked the best person he could think of, the little boy he had bullied. By the time Cameron moved on to middle school, their club had two hundred members at school who would meet during lunch on Fridays. Kids practice skills such as resisting peer pressure and asking for help. Cameron has spread his message even further and has spoken to organizations like the Boys & Girls Club of America and Boy Scouts of America about how to prevent bullying.

Yes, Cameron stopped bullying and apologized for his actions, but he did something more important—he worked to repair the harm he had caused. In doing so, both he and the little boy he teased were empowered to make a difference.

All young people are going to make mistakes. Young people will hurt others. They are going to break things. The question is: Are young people going to know how to put what has been broken back together? We can empower young people by helping them understand how they impact others, how to make it right, and how to practice and expect fairness.

Spark the Conversation

- Tell me about a time something was unfair.

- What does fairness mean?

- Why do kids get punished? What other responses can
  we have to wrongdoing?

We can't expect young people to act fairly if they don't understand what fairness means. Help young people develop a more sophisticated understanding of fairness by having conversations about real situations they have faced. Use those personal situations to help broaden their ideas about justice and equity.

A young person might say something like, "It's not fair that students can't talk in the hallways during passing period" or "It's not fair that I got grounded." Resist the urge to interject your own opinion. Instead, explore their reasoning. Have them explain exactly what about the situation they would like to see changed. Then try to steer the conversation from "I should be able to _____." to "All people should be able to _____." This is a great way to move a young person's thinking from the personal to the universal.

5

Effort and Confidence Matters

> I wish: That some adults
> Would understand That not
> every kid is useless.

My students are all eight or nine years old, and many have been lied to repeatedly but not necessarily explicitly. Some of my students come into my classroom believing they are stupid. That is a lie. They say things like, "I'm not good at math." That is a lie. One little boy was reading a book to me and couldn't figure out how to sound out one word. He turned to me as if he were confessing a secret and said, "Miss, I can't read. I'm not smart." That was a lie.

False claims like this happen so often that I have a response at the ready: "Who told you that lie?" In all the years I have asked children this question, not one has ever told me a name of someone who told them they were stupid. Perhaps a cruel child whispered it to them on the playground, or maybe a family member said it in a moment of frustration, but when I ask children to identify the person who told them they were stupid, they do not point out anyone in particular.

As a teacher, I have a very strict policy to take all claims of stupidity very seriously. It is just like bomb jokes at the airport. Every single self-insult is significant. Each time a child says, "I'm dumb," and you remain silent, you are providing confirmation of their own inferiority. I can't afford to miss one opportunity to challenge this type of destructive thinking because the consequences are disastrous.

Doubts about self-efficacy—the personal belief in your own abilities—are never benign. They are always malignant. If you believe you are inherently inferior to others, that belief will spread. It will affect every aspect of your life, every aspect of your learning and development. This is as true for adults as it is for children.

To combat this, I use myself as an example all the time. I don't try to cover up my mistakes; I shine a light on them. More often than I would like to admit, I make miscalculations while solving simple math problems in front of my entire class. One wonderful little quirk about third graders is the unparalleled joy they find in pointing out that their teacher forgot to borrow from the tens column. Gleeful students will shout out and tell me exactly what I did wrong. As a new teacher, I would ignore them entirely or just chuckle and say, "Oh, I was just testing you all to see who was paying attention." Then, I would move along. Now, however, I take every mistake as an opportunity. Feigning distress, I will say, "Oh no! I'm terrible at math! I'll never subtract correctly. Should

I just give up?" "No!" my students will shout back. Then we all cry out together, "Never give up! Never surrender!"

One day I took it to the next level. I grabbed a piece of construction paper and wrote, "I made a mistake, and it was awesome!" I hung it on the classroom door. Every time a student made a mistake or answered a question wrong, I invited them to pick out their favorite color of marker and sign the poster. Within a few days, the poster had taken on a life of its own. My students themselves would say, "Hey! Krissta made a mistake; she gets to sign the poster." When I made a mistake adding or subtracting during a math lesson, a chorus of children would say, "Miss! Go sign the poster." It became a physical representation of a growth mindset, the thinking that, with effort, one can improve.

Though I am committed to all my students believing in themselves, sometimes nothing I do helps. Sometimes it gets to a point where a teacher can't do anything at all. Sometimes the only person a child will believe is another child.

It happened one day when one of my students asked me for a piece of tape. Everyone in the class was finally quiet and working, and I figured he was just avoiding his assignment. So I told him no. The boy was insistent. "No, Miss, I need a piece of tape for this." He shoved a cupped hand in my face. In his hand sat a crumpled, torn corner of a piece of paper barely the size of a thumbnail. The note read, "yr smart."

Another kid in class had passed him that note, after he'd heard that boy say for the hundredth time, "I'm stupid. I can't do this." As I taped the tiny scrap of paper to his desk, the boy was beaming. The note wasn't a magic fix-all. He still struggled with self-confidence, but little by little we stopped hearing him say, "I'm stupid."

Try this . . .

WISE FEEDBACK

We can increase a sense of self-efficacy by increasing trust. This happens when we help young people believe our feedback is not merely criticism but rather based in a sincere belief that they have the ability to improve.

A study published in the *Journal of Experimental Psychology* examined how seventh-grade students responded to feedback on essays they wrote in a social studies course. When teachers' criticism was "accompanied by a message that conveyed high standards and assurances that they were confident the student could meet those standards, African American students were more than four times as likely to revise and resubmit the essay than if they received the criticism alone; this type of feedback also improved the quality of students' revisions."

FEEDBACK + ASSURANCES = IMPROVEMENT

EXAMPLES:

- Your previous math quizzes show me you have the skills to understand fractions. I know you can review the problems you got wrong, pay close attention to the numerator and denominator, and improve this assignment.

- I can tell from the way you speak to your brother and sister that you have the qualities of a great communicator. If you use this feedback on speaking clearly and directly, I know your presentation skills will improve.

- I know from what I have seen in practice that you have the ability to swim faster. If you take my feedback about your starting position and work on it for the next race, I know you can make your times faster.

Developing Confidence

It is tempting to believe that confidence is binary—there are confident kids and not-so-confident kids. That type of thinking is not only inaccurate but it also prevents our ability to help young people grow their level of confidence. Confidence is not something you are born with; confidence is something you develop.

Author and expert on child happiness, Maureen Healy, explains in *Psychology Today*, "Confidence actually can be derived from its Latin roots to be explained as 'with trust' or 'with faith' or 'with belief.' A confident child displays a belief in his or her own abilities. Such a belief is developed over time but hinges upon the ability to experience self-trust." When adults realize that confidence is indeed developed, we can play an active role in guiding young people in becoming secure and productive members of our communities.

Erik Erikson's "Psychosocial Stages of Development" theory has helped me see where my students are on a continuum of self-esteem. Erikson's theory breaks down personality development into eight developmental stages across a lifespan.

At each stage there is a key dichotomy that Erikson calls a crisis, such as trust and mistrust in infancy. If an infant's needs are met by a caring adult, the infant will trust the world; if the needs are not met, that infant will mistrust others, developing suspicion and fear. As a person grows, they move through subsequent developmental stages and will acquire virtues, or behaviors: first hope, then will, purpose, competence, and so on.

According to their age, the eight- and nine-year-olds in my classroom should theoretically be acquiring a sense of self-efficacy, or as Erikson calls it industriousness, during their third-grade year. Yet so many students are not. Why? Because they have not mastered the earlier developmental stages.

The little boy who told me he could not read is an example of this. He was easily embarrassed and discouraged, doubted his abilities at every turn, and never took initiative. At the beginning of the year, he had so much shame about his own abilities that he did not believe learning was even worth his effort. In terms of his psychosocial development and his level of confidence, that boy was closer to a preschool student than he was to his peers. He needed to be taught autonomy and initiative before he could develop self-confidence. With lots of help from his family, teachers, and peers, that boy began taking more pride in his work. He became more excited about lessons and was even able to support other students when they struggled.

There are so many kids like him out there. I am sure you know teenagers and adults who seem to struggle with confidence. Upon a closer look, it is not merely confidence they struggle with.

TABLE 5.1

ERIKSON'S PSYCHOSOCIAL STAGES ABBREVIATED

STAGE	CRISIS	VIRTUES
Infancy		
0–1 year	Trust vs. Mistrust	Hope
Early Childhood		
1–3 years	Autonomy vs. Shame	Will
Play age		
3–6 years	Initiative vs. Guilt	Purpose
School age		
6–12 years	Industry vs. Inferiority	Competence
Adolescence		
12–19 years	Identity vs. Confusion	Fidelity

Follow the chain of development to see where it is broken. Trust leads to independence, which leads to initiative and self-control. Then and only then can a person develop confidence. If we want students to feel empowered to learn, grow, and make a difference in the world, we need to meet young people where they are and fill in the developmental gaps.

Reflecting on Our Own Confidence

Confidence can often be a double-edged sword for young people. Adults tell young people all the time "believe in yourself" and "always try your best." But what happens to a young person who does believe in themselves and does try their best? What reactions does a child who has a genuine and robust sense of confidence experience? I had an insightful conversation with my friend Joseph Mathews, a professor of education at Hunter College.

Joseph told me that as a child, he always had an intrinsic confidence. He thought he looked good. He knew he had musical and athletic talents. He had skills. But in school, he was surrounded by people who were uncomfortable with that confidence.

Joseph learned at a young age that it was unacceptable to express pride in himself at school. "In the classroom, I could not say, 'I'm a great reader.' The instant I said that, my friends, my peers, even my teachers would tell me to not be so full of myself, calm down, be more humble." Every mistake he made, every word he had to sound out, every wrong answer was used as evidence that his positive view of himself was flawed. "Saying you were good at something was like putting a target on your back. Others couldn't wait to shoot you down," he recounted.

This treatment led Joseph to stop flaunting his abilities and stop trying to succeed in school. As a result, his grades were terrible. "That's when teachers stepped in to scold me for not putting in effort. That's when principals made overtures about the importance of staying in school. They wanted to build me up but only after they had broken my spirit."

How many kids are like Joseph? How many kids are walking a tightrope, encouraged to act confident but warned not be too confident? It's hard enough for young people to feel confident in the first place, and it's even harder to express that confidence in just the right way so it is not threatening to others.

Joseph became a teacher and credits having a larger purpose and an outlet for his gifts as a way to restore his own confidence. Now he teaches education majors and asks his students—all future teachers—point blank, "Are you confident? Do you believe in yourself?" Are you confident enough to express it to others?" Overwhelmingly, the answer is "No."

That's when Joseph realized, "Confidence breeds confidence. Insecurity breeds insecurity." "Many of these future educators had been socialized to play down their talents and confidence while they were students themselves. And if they do not learn to be comfortable with expressing their confidence, they will teach their students insecurity." Joseph helps to these future teachers understand that their own sense of confidence and self worth must be in tact before they step into a classroom. I had my own experience with this.

When I was in fifth grade, I was reading some little worksheet out loud to my teacher. I understood everything I was reading but tripped over the words when I said them out loud. My teacher made the comment, "You aren't very good at reading aloud are you?" At the time, I just agreed. Whenever I read something to a group or a class and I misspoke, that little thought popped into my head, "I'm just not very good at reading aloud." It never occurred to me to challenge that thinking.

A decade later, I started reading storybooks aloud to the class as a student teacher. I tripped over words and had to go back and reread sentences. It was embarrassing that I couldn't even read a kid's book correctly to a room full of seven-year-olds. I mentioned it to my lead teacher, Rachel Bernard. I asked her how I could get better because reading aloud is something I had always struggled with. A teacher had even noticed it once, I confided. She smiled and replied, "Isn't it funny how a little comment can stick with us like that?"

Hearing that question made me rethink everything. This whole time, I believed I had a deficiency. I was told it was hard for me to read aloud, and I accepted it as fact. And whenever I did read aloud and stumbled over a word, my brain would jump to the idea that I'm not good at this, which made it even harder to focus on the sentences and say the words correctly. I would stumble even more, thus providing proof to myself and everyone listening that I, indeed, was bad at reading aloud. But was any of it even true?

I made a decision right then and there to think differently. I chose to look at the mountain of evidence that told me I was, in reality, a proficient reader, and ignore a careless sentence a teacher had once said to me.

Let me tell you, I am excellent at reading aloud. I choose books kids fall in love with. I do all the voices of the characters. I act out the story and jump up on tables as I read. And I know just how to hold the tension before a big cliffhanger. But I do trip over a word or misread sentences. You know what? That actually makes me even better at reading aloud to children because it gives me the opportunity to model my thought process as a reader. I say, "Wait a minute. That doesn't make sense, let me go back and check the sounds in the words," and "Hold on, that word says running not raining, let me reread it so I understand it." Each time that I do this kids are not only enjoying a story, but they are getting a peek inside the mind of a proficient reader.

Examining my own confidence as a reader has taught me important lessons. First, as adults we may still be believing lies told to us in childhood that are not based in reality. When a moment of self-doubt presents itself, confront it. Ask yourself where it stems from and if it's even true. Eradicate the self-talk that doesn't serve you so that you are not modeling self-doubt for the young people in your life. My own personal mantra is: it's never too late to stop the self-hate.

Second, kids remember each of those little comments long after we have forgotten them. As Joseph says, "Be thoughtful with your words. Children are listening. Everyday, there is a child who uses the words of a thoughtless adult as evidence they won't make it. But there is also a child who succeeds because someone gave a word of encouragement."

I wish..... I hade a big sisthen? to halp me with my homework

Children who struggle with confidence often believe their effort doesn't matter. They believe they are inherently inferior to others and this stops them from developing a strong sense of self-efficacy.

As caring adults, our words and our actions make a huge difference. That is what happened for third-grade student Anaya Ellick of Chesapeake, Virginia, when her principal, Tracy Cox, encouraged her to enter a handwriting contest. Anaya ended up winning a national prize after putting in a great deal of effort to perfect her penmanship. "She is a hard worker," Cox explained. "She is determined. She is independent. She is a vivacious and a no-excuses type of young lady."

Anyone who wins national recognition is an inspiration, but Anaya's story goes deeper. She was born without fingers or

Try this . . .

LADDER AND SLIDE

Every day we experience challenges and successes, big and small. I wanted a quick way for my students to reflect on this. I heard of a strategy called roses and thorns where a person states their rose, the highlight of the day, and their thorn, something that went wrong. But that metaphor wasn't quite right for my purposes.

I wanted a concept that kids could relate to. I also wanted to represent challenges differently. Challenges are natural and even useful parts of our day, not dangerous, sharp objects to avoid. I came up with the idea of ladder and slide.

The ladder, I explain to my students, is when you have to climb, you have to work hard. It's the effort you had to put in. The slide, on the other hand, is the joyful ride. It's the part of the day that felt easy and free. It's a moment when your hard work has paid off. My students will quickly whip around into a circle and share their own personal ladder and slide of the day.

This simple metaphor sends the message to kids that each and every one of us has to put in effort. There are parts of everyone's day that seem laborious and challenging. That is a good thing. We all put in the effort for a reason. There is a reward waiting for us. You will never get to the slide unless you put in the work to climb the ladder. The higher the climb, the longer the slide.

thumbs. She writes by balancing a pencil between the ends of her arms. Challenges didn't stop Anaya. "I'll be able to do it, if I try," she explained. She saw her effort pay off again, when a year later she won a second national prize for handwriting—this time for writing in cursive. Anaya's success is a great example to us all. We can choose to build up young people.

We can offer constant reassurance when they experience a crisis of confidence. We can help frame struggles as challenges, not as proof of inferiority. This is how young people realize their ideas and efforts matter. When young people have this understanding they start to recognize their power to make a difference in the world.

I wish for safety and security world wide.

Spark the Conversation

- Why do some people give up and some people persist?

- What would help you feel more confident?

- Are there things you believe about yourself that are
  not true?

- Who inspires you to do your best?

We all want young people to persist in problem solving. As caring adults, we can have an impact, even before a challenge arises. If we have open and consistent dialogue about frustrations and hardships, we can also talk about strategies that help people overcome difficulties.

It's also important to normalize the idea that everyone goes through challenges and everyone has had a crisis of confidence. We can point to examples in books and TV shows. We can use examples of inspirational athletes and historical figures, but more powerfully we can point to our own everyday experiences.

6

Powerful Perceptions

I WISH... I can tutor kids with math and Science so they can do good on ther home wors and get good scores.

You just failed a test. Your project ended terribly. You were not accepted into the program. Whose fault is it?

Your answer reveals your causal thinking. Psychology professor Dr. Raymond P. Perry explains, "In trying to make sense of life's circumstances, people employ causal thinking to identify explanations for their successes and failures." With causal thinking, the central question is: What *causes* life's achievements and challenges?

Basically, if you think your own actions and beliefs are responsible for your successes and failures you have what researchers call "high perceived control." You passed the test because you studied. You did not finish the project because you procrastinated. You are in control over life's outcomes. It is your high perception of control that leads you to have a resilient mindset.

In contrast, if you think your own beliefs and actions do not influence life's outcomes, you are a person with low perceived control. You passed the test because it was easy and the teacher likes you. You didn't finish the project because there wasn't enough time. You are not in control over life's outcomes. Your low perception of control leads you to have a helpless mindset.

This is not to ignore or minimize very real issues of bias that exist in schools and other institutions. It is unreasonable to ask the victim of discrimination to take personal responsibility for the failures of oppressive systems. That being said, we can still learn from decades of research that has shown how causal thinking impacts our lives. Perry even found that "Older adults who ascribe health challenges to 'old age' (uncontrollable causes) have shorter lifespans." In school, a student with a helpless mindset does not believe they have any control over their learning, which in turn makes it more difficult to respond to and overcome academic challenges. For example, if a student thinks a class is just too hard for them, they are less likely to go to the tutoring session. If a student believes the teacher will score them unfairly, they will put less effort into writing their essay.

What's more, the helpless mindset not only makes it difficult for the student to take steps to improve their learning, but it also develops a psychological profile that makes it more difficult to receive help from others. Researchers found that so-called helpless students are "in need of enriched educational opportunities such as effective instruction but are unlikely to derive the academic benefits that normally accrue in such learning conditions." This means we cannot teach our way out of problems caused by low perceived power.

We must help children recognize the control and power they have in life.

Be Coachable

Often, my students have an unhelpful pattern of thinking that starts as soon as I step in to help. They think, "The teacher is helping me. I must not get it. If I don't understand, I must be stupid. I hate this." It's a quick and slippery slope. I can see a sense of helplessness in their faces. Sometimes this thinking leads kids to become oppositional. If they can pick a fight with me, they can avoid tasks that will make them feel unsuccessful. Avoidant strategies range from frequent bathroom breaks to disappearing notebooks. One year a student, who was perfectly capable of writing, started the year out by physically hiding under tables hoping to go unnoticed. Too often these behaviors are labeled as disrespect or laziness, when in reality the child is communicating they need our help to develop a more resilient mindset.

In my classroom, I use the word "coachable." Kids understand that even incredible athletes work with coaches to improve. I want my students to realize that being coached is not a sign of inferiority, it's necessary for anyone to grow and develop. In national survey of more than one hundred college basketball coaches ranked the top characteristics of coachable athletes as:

1. Willingness to be coached

2. Willingness to sacrifice for the team

3. Acceptance of criticism

4. Acceptance of individual role

It is interesting that willingness and acceptance are at the very top of the coaches' list. Sometimes we think young people will naturally develop these skills, but often adults need to explicitly teach these skills. I have my students generate a list of what a coachable student looks like, sounds like, acts like, and thinks like. They say things like:

Coachable students

- show their work to the teacher

- ask questions to make sure they understand

- say, "Now I realize _____" and "Next time I will _____."

- set goals and monitor their progress

- use mistakes to learn

- understand we are all working hard to improve

Helping young people define a coachable mindset can help them understand the role they play in their own learning and their own work. When young people understand their effort matters, they perceive themselves as in control of their own successes.

Sense of Power

Just like control, power is a matter of perception. How we acknowledge our own power has big implications. Researchers at the University of California Berkeley sought to understand an individual's sense of power, which they defined as "the perception of one's ability to influence another person or other people."

The results are fascinating and demonstrate that "those who perceive themselves as powerful behave in more effective ways that increase their actual power." Just believing you have power helps you get power! This is one reason why the most confident candidate, not always the most qualified candidate, usually gets the job.

Perhaps the most exciting information is that we adults can have a very real impact on a young person's sense of power. I have always felt instinctively that if I can help students feel worthy, confident, and powerful inside the walls of my classroom, then they can carry this with them outside of school. Research shows that instinct is right.

I reached out to Dr. Cameron Anderson, one of the researchers who conducted the sense of power studies. He explained that in the laboratory context, when participants "had a higher sense of power in a prior social group, they feel that same sense of power in the new social group. These carry-over effects are in short-term laboratory contexts but still suggest that if you make someone feel powerful in one relationship, this will boost their feelings of power in other relationships."

The ripple effect to empowering children travels beyond your own relationship with a child. When you give a child a high sense of power, that translates to actions that manifest actual power.

We adults are not off the hook here. As adults, our own sense of power can determine whether or not we are effective communicators and caregivers.

In one study, researchers recruited mothers of elementary-aged children to participate in a study where they taught a child a computer game. Before the teaching session, the mothers were measured on their level of perceived personal power. Even though, as mothers, the participants had tremendous power over children who are indeed very dependent on them, some of the mothers viewed themselves as what researchers referred to as "powerless parents."

These "powerless parents" were less effective in teaching the computer game to children. They were more likely to use a "communication style that is typically seen as unclear, untrustworthy, and potentially condescending." Researchers noted the communication style used by the "powerless parents" was likely to lead to "an escalating pattern of misunderstanding and conflict."

All of this means that if you are a caring adult, whether you're a parent, teacher, coach, or mentor, you must recognize your own power over children. When you are in this role, you provide everything from safety, nutrition, and guidance. You hold so much information and power. Own that power.

Some adults see themselves as lacking power. They attribute issues to a child's personality or disposition. We have all heard some version of "I can't get him to do his chores, he is just so stubborn," and "She is just so careless and bad at spelling, she will never pass those quizzes." I have even heard a mother say of a child who was not yet two years old, "She is just throwing a fit because she is trying make me mad. She does this all the time."

This type of thinking does not serve us, and it certainly does not serve the young people in our lives. Perhaps the child who refuses to do his chores needs to have a system that holds him accountable. Perhaps the careless speller needs more instruction in phonics. And perhaps the toddler is hungry or tired and is just trying to get her needs met.

In each of those scenarios, adults absolved themselves of the responsibility to guide a child in problem solving. It's an easy mistake. I've done it myself.

Try this . . .

RETRAIN YOUR BRAIN

When we have incorrect perceptions about our own power, we train our brains to think we are not in control over our successes and failures. The good news is we can retrain our brains to see more accurately how our actions and choices impact our lives.

For decades, researchers have seen the impact of a simple strategy called attributional retraining. It focuses on what a person attributes outcomes to. For example, a grade on a test might be attributed to many things like the effectiveness of the teacher, the difficulty of the subject matter, the amount of time spent studying, or the intellect of the student.

In a study, participants, all college students, watched a video that "encouraged students to attribute poor performance to lack of effort and emphasized that the amount of effort that a person expends is not a stable trait, but is actually controllable." The video also emphasized changing study strategies to fit the needs of each different course. Then participants discussed the video. At the conclusion of the study, researchers found students who watched these videos had an average grade of a B while students who did not had an average grade of a C+. Attributional retraining studies have been replicated many times and have found that this strategy

(Continues)

(TRY THIS, Power Recall Cont.)

"helps students reframe the way they think about success and failure by encouraging them to take responsibility for academic outcomes and adopt the "can-do" attitude."
   Here are some examples of retaining your thoughts.

Instead of thinking _____.	Think _____.
I'm just not smart enough to pass this math test.	I was successful in other classes, but the strategies I used before are not working anymore. I need to find another way to study. I can ask my teacher for help figuring out a study strategy that works for me.
I lost the student government election. I'm just not good enough. What's the point of trying?	Losing the election can help me see what I can do differently. Waiting to the last minute to put up posters and write my speech did not work. I should think of new ways to communicate my ideas for the next election.

I still remember one of the first lessons I ever taught as a student teacher. I remember it well because it was a total disaster. None, and I mean none, of the kids were paying attention. They weren't raising their hands to answer my questions. Some were even rolling around on the floor. One kid even shoved a pencil into the heating unit, which made an irritating, clunking noise for the rest of the day. No one was learning anything.

At the end of that brutal lesson, I debriefed with my mentor teacher, Rachel Bernard. She started off by asking me an easy question, "How do you think it went?"

"Terribly! The kids were not paying attention, they didn't care at all. It was awful," I responded.

She asked knowingly, "Why?"

That was another easy question. "It's snowing, so they couldn't go outside for recess. They were completely wound up. None of them could sit still, and they refused to pay attention to me."

"So, what could you have done differently?" Rachel asked kindly.

I was taken aback. What could *I* do? This wasn't about me. I was teaching. I was following the lesson plan I had written. I was doing my part. It was the kids who weren't doing their part. Again I explained, "They had inside recess today. Kids need recess or they won't be able to pay attention. It's snowing, I can't control the weather!"

With more patience than I deserved she said, "Well, we live in Colorado. It's probably going to snow again. What are you going to do differently next time?"

It was so convenient for me to attribute my disaster of a lesson to the snow, the inside recess, and all that excess energy. It was easy to see all the parts that were outside of my control, it was a lot harder to recognize my role in the fiasco. True, it is hard for kids who have been sitting still all day long to pay attention, but I chose to do nothing to address the situation.

Rachel helped me think through some easy solutions, solutions that seem pretty obvious looking back. I could play a game in the classroom that got the kids moving. I could put on a song and host a mini dance party or play a round of Simon Says. No, I cannot control the weather, but my choices on those dreaded inside recess days are powerful.

If we give our power away, we are unable to be a positive influence. By perceiving ourselves as less powerful than we actually are, we become worse caregivers, worse communicators, and worse teachers. You have a great deal of power and influence. By recognizing this truth, you can be more effective in guiding young people to develop their own sense of power.

> I wish Story
> I wish I did not have ADhD it is to frustrating. And sometime it is hard to bo math becaue you have to conentrate on math. Another reason is my ADhD duesnt allow me to focus or pey attentios for a long time. So I have found some way to help me wiht focus ant pay attention in class. I have noon cusnion that sits on my chair for me to and do my work, I also five minutes breenlss tohelp my refresh my brain. These are all my reason I do not want ADhD in the wold.

Try this . . .

POWER RECALL

In a study led by Adam Galinsky of Northwestern University, researchers asked a basic question: Does power lead to action? Through a series of experiments they were able to demonstrate empirically that people who feel powerful are more likely to take action.

Researchers divided participants into two groups—high-power and low-power. They asked the high-power group to think of a time in their lives when they had power over others and write a short essay about it. Conversely, the low-power group was asked to recall a time when others had power over them and write about that. Then participants were led to individual rooms. In the room, the researchers placed a very cold fan blowing directly at the participant's face. They found that "High-power participants were more than twice as likely to take action against the fan as to ignore it."

The only difference between the two groups was whether they thought about a powerful or a powerless experience. Researchers call this phenomenon mind-set priming. Just the act of thinking about a time you were powerful can lead you to take action, even a simple action like moving an annoying fan. We can use this strategy with young people. Simply have young people discuss or write about a time they had power. Here are some questions to get you started.

(Continues)

(TRY THIS, Power Recall Cont.)

Think about a time you had power, a time when you could control if someone else got something, or a time when you could help someone.

- What happened?

- What actions did you take?

- What decisions did you make?

- What did it feel like to be in control?

What's Your Part?

At the park one day, I watched my friend Rachael Roe respond to her toddler who had fallen and was crying. She acknowledged that her daughter was in pain and wrapped her arms around the girl to comfort her. Then she said this, "You fell on the step because you were running fast and not looking. If you don't want to fall again, slow down and look at your feet." I realized the impact of this small exchange. Rachael followed a simple format: pay attention to the problem, recognize your role in it, and make a change. She opted to model this strategy for her daughter instead of just kissing a boo-boo. When we can help children understand their role in outcomes, even as simple as falling down, we help them see the power of their own choices.

I do something similar in my classroom. Two of the most used phrases in my classroom are simply, "Notice this" and "What's your part?"

At least once every morning a student comes up to me, beaming and shoving a crinkled reading log in my face and says, "Look Miss! I did my homework!" I don't ignore this or say something dismissive like, "Well, you are supposed to do your homework anyway." I always jump on the chance to say, "Notice this! How do you feel? You feel proud when you do your homework." I am more excited by their pride in reading than the completed homework itself.

I use another quick strategy that I call "Name Emojis." I train kids that whenever they write their name on a paper in my class to draw a little emoji next to it showing how they feel. As you can imagine, I get a lot of sleepy emojis in the morning, several happy emojis, and usually one or two sad and angry little faces. Just the act of noticing your own emotions throughout the day is powerful. These little Name Emojis create a habit of self-monitoring your emotions, helps me know when to respond to the needs of a sad or anxious child, and also gives insight into how my students' emotions are affecting their classwork.

Sometimes, a group of students will walk by our classroom talking loudly and will disrupt my students who are working. In a school with hundreds of children, this is bound to happen. When I can, I point this out to kids. "Notice this. How do you feel? It's frustrating when you are trying to read and other kids are loud in the hall." Then, when it's my students who are the ones being too rambunctious in the hallway, I say, "Notice this. It was frustrating when other people distracted you. Now you are distracting others," or even "Notice this. It feels a little embarrassing when the principal has to tell big kids like you how to behave in the hallway."

To be honest, I also say things like, "Don't forget to turn in your homework," and "Stop talking in the hallway." But I try as much as I can to draw a child's attention to their own choices. It is a slow process, yet inviting children to pause and notice their feelings is a worthy endeavor. It helps children connect actions to outcomes.

My classroom is not a blissed-out campfire, kumbaya circle. In a classroom where twenty-five to thirty humans spend most of the day, conflict is inevitable. There are problems of all shapes and sizes that come up during each school day. One of the best ways to resolve interpersonal conflict and to help children understand their role in it is the simple yet powerful question my principal Jodie Carrigan uses often with students: "What's your part?"

One afternoon, my math class was interrupted by a child who began hyperventilating in sobs. It turns out that a girl named Ginni had walked over to a little boy and told him, "Dakota told me that she doesn't like you and doesn't want to be your friend." The boy was inconsolable. While he was calming down, I called Ginni out into the hallway. The first thing out of her mouth was a list of reasons why she shouldn't be the one in trouble, that she liked the boy and was his friend, and that indeed all of this was caused by Dakota who said something very mean. I didn't challenge her. I just asked, "What's Dakota's part?" Immediately Ginni recounted the whole story and the mean thing that Dakota said. I took a beat. "Ok, so what's your part?"

Ginni looked at me confused, mouth agape. She told again how Dakota had said something very mean and that was the reason the boy was crying. I again asked her, "That is Dakota's part.

What's *your* part?" Eventually, Ginni was able to own that her role was hearing something mean and then taking it upon herself to walk over and tell the boy something mean. The first step to resolving the problem was for Ginni to be aware of the power of her choices.

These two little phrases—"Notice this" and "What's your part?"—are not only effective with little children. Young people of all ages can also benefit from pausing and recognizing their reactions as well as being accountable to themselves for their choices. We all can become more powerful when we identify our role in life's successes and failures. Responsibility increases our sense of power.

Spark the Conversation

- Do you think of yourself as a powerful person? Why or why not?

- Think about a time you were successful. What actions did you take that made you successful?

- If someone fails at something, what should they do?

For each of us, it's pretty easy to congratulate ourselves when things are going well. It's doesn't take much psychological effort to explain why we got a good grade, won the game, or got our proposal past the committee. We can point to our abilities, our effort, and our drive. It can be lot harder to claim personal responsibility for our failures.

When helping a young person reflect on a particular challenge, it's important to acknowledge the reality. In every situation there are factors beyond their control and factors within their control. Help them identify both. Say a young person got a bad grade, lost the match, or had their proposal rejected. Validate their frustration especially when it comes to the forces working against them and outside of their control but use an "and also" approach so that young person sees their own role.

The teacher does grade harshly *and also* I could have proofread my essay more carefully. The referee made bad calls *and also* my serve needs to be more accurate. The committee was not initially in favor of my proposal *and also* I could have addressed their concerns in a more detailed way.

Ruminating on a failure will not change the outcome, but taking personal responsibility for your own actions and decisions will provide a path forward.

7

Real Kids, Real Results

I WISH... I can create an organi-zation that donates supplies to school I wish this because some schools don't have school supplies and all students should be able to have pencils, crayons and paper.

I was in student government in high school. In some ways, it resembled a real government. Students campaigned for offices, and we held an election. But the actual work we did was nothing like a government. We did no governing. Instead, we planned homecoming events and school dances. We hosted fundraisers and pep rallies. Our student government had absolutely no influence on school policies.

Don't get me wrong, I enjoyed being a part of the organization. It helped me build confidence and has resulted in lifelong friendships. I'm grateful that the program was offered and the school dedicated resources to it, but I do lament the opportunity that was missed. There was a group of teenagers who said, "We want to be a leaders, we want to contribute, we want to make decisions." And we did, but only in superficial ways.

My hope is that when young people say, "I want to lead, I want to make a difference," they are taken seriously and encouraged. In order for children to step up and become leaders, adults need to share how things actually change by explaining the mechanisms of power in our society.

I WISH... I wish could help zoo by donating money to anial care. I wish this so They scan buy food for all animals and the exhits care better.

Try this . . .
POWER MAPPING

I joined a community group called Equity Network United for Denver (ENUF Denver), which is focused on improving education for local students. One problem we identified is that in Colorado our schools are woefully, embarrassingly underfunded. We knew that a local tax measure was up for a vote and, if it passed, desperately needed funds would be sent to schools, so we made it our goal to help it get passed. In order to gain support we needed to identify allies and stakeholders. This is when I learned the power mapping strategy.

Power mapping is a visual tool used primarily by community organizers and non-profits. It helps identify key stakeholders that can either help or deter your efforts. There are a few popular variations of the power map, but the one we used had a simple x and y axis.

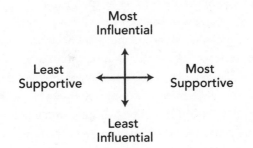

The vertical y-axis ranged from most influential at the top to least influential at the bottom. The horizontal x-axis ranged from strongly oppose at the left to strongly support at the right.

Then we set about plotting stakeholders on the chart. Just identifying stakeholders was illuminating. Of course I knew that the school board members, families of students, the teachers union, and the superintendent were all stakeholders as they had a vested interest in the quality of our schools. But I learned our education funding was also influenced by forces such as the oil and gas industry, former mayors, and a local billionaire.

(Continues)

(TRY THIS, Power Mapping Cont.)

For each stakeholder we identified, we used our collective knowledge to categorize their level of support and their level of influence. We focused our efforts on stakeholders who had a high level of support and also a high level of influence. If we could convince these stakeholders to partner with us, it would have a big impact.

Young people can use power mapping too. For example, say a group of young people want healthier food offerings in the school cafeteria. Students likely think the principal of a school has 100 percent control over this decision. That is just not true. If those students focus their efforts on persuading the principal, they won't get very far. There are other important stakeholders. The families of students, cafeteria staff, teachers, custodians, the district nutrition department, the school board, the multibillion-dollar school lunch industry, and the U.S. Department of Agriculture that administers the national school lunch program are all key stakeholders to consider.

With younger children, you can use one axis in isolation to help them understand what levels of influence means or which stakeholders would support versus oppose your plan.

I wish that people stop smoking because its bad for your body.

The Results

When Girl Scout troop 789 asked city council member Charles Richardson of Aurora, Colorado, to meet, he didn't quite know what he was in for. "I was, frankly, thinking it would be a resolution adopting a city insect or bird or flower. This was something much bigger," he told the *Washington Post*.

The thirteen- and fourteen-year-old Girl Scouts wanted to make an impact, not through naming an official animal, but through fighting against toxic chemicals. The troop had just earned a badge by researching air pollution and learning about the dangers of third-hand smoke, when chemicals and toxins build up on surfaces like countertops and car seats. They also found out that, even though the dangerous effects exposing a child to smoke in an enclosed space were well known, it was perfectly legal in their city to smoke in a car with a child present.

As Makenna Batcho, then thirteen years old, recounted, "We wanted to keep kids safe from being exposed to dangerous chemicals. One of the girls had the idea of passing a law banning smoking in cars with kids. Honestly, I wasn't sure it was possible, but I figured it was worth a try."

The first step was to win the support of Councilmember Richardson, who was eager to help because his wife had been exposed to smoke as a child and had likely developed asthma as a result. He told the troop they would need to gather research and create a proposal. "It was clear from the beginning that no one would go easy on us just because we were kids. If we wanted a real ordinance passed we would have to go through the same legislative process as anyone else," explained Makenna. The troop reached out to a tobacco treatment specialist at a local hospital who testified to the impact that smoke inhalation has on children. They met with the city attorney and drafted up an ordinance. After feedback from the council, they amended their ordinance to make the punishment a fine or community service.

Finally, at a city council meeting the ordinance went to a vote. Five were in favor, five were against. When the mayor cast the deciding vote, the Girl Scout troop officially achieved its goal of passing the first ordinance in Colorado to ban smoking in a car with a child present.

"Most of my friends are passionate about something, but they don't always take action," said Makenna. "I think it's because they don't realize they really do have the power to make a difference in their community. They just need someone to believe in them and help them through the process."

The troop learned how to navigate the real mechanisms of power in their community. They were able to leverage a relationship with their council member and form a coalition with community members. They had to negotiate and compromise so that their proposal would earn support. No one told the girls their ideas were too lofty or that they should wait until they are older. They were empowered.

So was Cassandra Lin. As a fifth-grade student, Cassandra began learning about climate change and the environmental effects of burning fossil fuel. "I promised myself that I would do everything in my power to try and stop this rising problem," said Cassandra. Then she learned that cooking oil could be recycled to heat homes and realized people in her community were struggling to pay for heat during the harsh winters.

Together with her friends, Cassandra created a community service team called Project TGIF, meaning Turn Grease into Fuel. They started by raising awareness about recycling cooking oil and eventually persuaded the town council in Westerly, Rhode

Island, to establish cooking oil collection stations. The children then convinced local restaurants to donate their used oil for recycling. All the collected oil is sent to a local biofuel refiner. Once processed, it is sent back out as fuel to families in need who use it to heat their homes. This was a win-win-win situation for environmentalists, businesses, and residents.

Cassandra and her friends already made a difference in their community. Their biofuel heated 575 homes, but they didn't stop there. They were able to accomplish something that adult environmentalists had been attempting unsuccessfully for years. They drafted and helped to introduce a state bill that mandated all Rhode Island businesses recycle their grease instead of dumping it. In 2011, the governor signed into law the Used Cooking Oil Recycling Act.

The work continued. Cassandra and her friends conducted a nationwide survey and lab tests to prove that biofuel was more reliable, cleaner, safer, and cheaper than gasoline. They took their finding to their school board. The superintendent made the decision to use biodiesel to fuel all the school buses in the district's fleet.

"I want to challenge you all to find what it is that you're passionate about, that makes you excited and motivates you," says Cassandra. "It can be anything, whether it is volunteering, sports, reading, anything! I challenge you to go out and do it. Use your energy for good. Who knows, you might even change the world!"

Cassandra and her friends could have stopped at raising awareness. They could have put up a few posters about recycling oil and changed their personal habits. But, instead, they collaborated with real institutions, the town council, the late legislature, and the school board to make lasting, sustainable change.

Try This . . .

FWFWFLFH

There is a community organizing strategy called FWFWFLFH, which stands for Fight, Win, Fight, Win, Fight, Lose, Fight Harder. It means to start your efforts with small, winnable goals. It also means to treat those smaller efforts in the same manner you would approach larger, more complex efforts.

For example, imagine a group of students want to reduce waste in school cafeterias. They want to have a zero waste policy where all biodegradable material is composted, packaging is recycled, and single-use items such as plastic spoons are eliminated. A small, winnable goal might be getting a recycle bin placed in the lunchroom.

Even if they know their school will easily agree to put out a recycling bin when asked, the students should still implement strategies like writing an official request, recruiting fellow students to attend a meeting, and negotiating with the school administration over when and where the recycling bins are placed. The goal of all this work is not only to obtain the recycling bin, but also to teach the organization the process of making change. So when they set their sights on more challenging targets like setting up a composting system or replacing single-use plastic forks, the group has built the skill set it will need to get the job done.

Caring adults can help young people identify the smaller goals that build up to larger goals. We can help young people prioritize their efforts and start with tasks that will earn momentum-building wins. It's also important that we emphasize learning the strategies used to create change such as hosting meetings, recruiting members, and communicating their concerns. Practicing that process in smaller steps will help young people create larger successes in the future.

I wish that littering was not a problem
So animals could live better.

Share Your Why

Why do you want this to change? Why is it so important to you? Why does this work matter?

When a young person wants to work for change, these are the types of questions they should reflect on. Asking *why* helps clarify the motivation and the hope behind the work. It is also a perfect way to prompt storytelling.

Storytelling is a powerful force in creating change. It is how we connect an issue with real people. One popular framework for storytelling was developed by Marshall Ganz, who is a veteran activist, an organizer, and now a Harvard professor. It is called the public narrative. Ganz explains, "Stories speak the language of emotion, the language of the heart; they not only teach us how we 'ought to' act, but they can also inspire us with the 'courage to' act." The public narrative has three components: the story of self, the story of us, and the story of now.

To create a public narrative, young people start with their own stories. They should identify the experiences that motivate them to work for change. Why have I been moved to leadership on this issue? Then, the public narrative moves into the story of us. Think about what common values and experiences the community shares. What goals can we all work toward? The final component is the story of now. This should describe an urgent challenge and also should give a clear way to take action.

Several years ago, I wanted to see a change in my school district. I realized that my students had diverse family make-ups but schools were not using inclusive language to describe those families. Specifically, I wanted the district to change the term used in official communication from "parent-teacher conferences" to "family conferences." It took three years and a stack of emails to more departments than I care to count, but the board of education voted to make the change officially in 2018.

Below is an example of my public narrative in the Self-Us-Now format:

As a child, I remember getting up one day when it was still dark out. My parents worked late and had a long commute, so my teacher allowed my mother to come in before school for a conference. I'm a teacher now, and several times a year I have similar meetings with my students and their families. These types of meetings have been called parent-teacher conferences for as long as I can remember, but that name doesn't accurately describe what happens. Many times I, the teacher, meet with parents. But other times I meet with grandmothers, aunts and uncles, or older siblings. That is because some of my students are not being raised by their parents. This reality can be painful, especially for my students who are grieving the death of a parent or have experienced harm at the hands of a parent. I don't want any of my students to feel that their families are not acceptable. I don't want grandmothers and uncles who are loving caregivers to feel like they are exceptions to a rule.

We all love our families. We know that families play such a sacred role in education. We all want kids to know their families, no matter what form they take, are honored and validated at their school.

My school decided to use the term "family conferences," and this change should be made district wide. I have asked the calendar committee use the term "Family Conferences" rather than "Parent-Teacher Conferences" on the official academic calendar so that all of our students and their families feel included. Will you send an email to the committee members expressing your desire to see inclusive family language used throughout our school district? Will you join me in asking for this small yet important change?

I wish bullying would stop happening around the world. I wish bullying would stop happening because its been causing serious problems. I would like to make an impacket by putting up posters and spreading the word around the world.

MY POWER

Salem Atsbha Hailu,
fifteen-year-old student

We sat at the bottom of the school steps. I looked at my sister, and my sister looked at me. She said, "I'll do it, if you do it." I replied, "I'll do it, if you do it." And that's how we started our campaigns for student government. A few weeks later, we had both become the class presidents of our respective grade levels.

As soon as I took office, the pressure was on. Everyone who voted for me wanted me to deliver on my campaign promise. Most of all, I was excited to create change, and I put pressure on myself. I needed to figure out a way to change the dress code, quickly.

For years, our complaints about the dress code had fallen on deaf ears. We were dismissed as nothing more than teenagers whining about uniforms. But this was about more than fashion. We felt the dress code was rooted in a narrow view of what a professional or an academic looks like. Wearing expensive shirts and khakis does not make me a better student; it just makes me more palatable to the dominant culture. We saw an injustice that needed to be corrected.

As pressure mounted, I was anxious to deliver, and my first attempt was the petition. It went exactly as expected. Quickly, more than two hundred students signed, all demanding change to the dress code. I figured most of the work was done. I would present the petition to the administration, request a couple meetings, make my case, and that would be it. I learned that change does not come that easily.

Looking back, I can see my naïveté. I had misunderstandings about the hierarchy of power when it came to dress code at our school network. I also had misconceptions about what people in positions of power at our school were capable of. I was patiently informed by our student government advisor, Ms. Couture, that my petition was meaningless. There were no rules or processes by which to consider petitions. I was informed by the school dean that he was not responsible for the dress code policy and had no power to change it. I realized that I had acted out of my own accord and did not consider all the facts. I did not form any sort of coalition and did not seek partnership with the groups or organizations that supported the cause.

I felt defeated, even foolish. I could have easily given up and spent my year as class president planning school dances. But I was raised by a strong Ethiopian mother who taught me quitting was not an option. She taught me to learn from my mistakes and speak up if something is not right.

As a student government, we decided to take a step back. Yes, we were eager to make an impact, but we needed to first create structures and systems. If anything was going to change, we needed to write bylaws that would answer basic questions like: Do we vote openly or

(Continues)

(MY POWER, Salem Atsbha Hailu Cont.)

anonymously? Who can call for a vote? How many votes are needed to win?

While I saw the value in building this governmental framework, my classmates were not so patient. Some vocal students were calling for an all-out rebellion. Their plan was to lead the entire student body in a protest by unilaterally breaking the dress code. After all, the school couldn't possibly give every single student detention.

I saw the passion behind their plan, but I also saw the greater implications. If we tried to force the school's hand, the students and the administration would instantly become adversaries. We risked losing any of the power we were building in student government.

I told my classmates they needed to hold their own perspective accountable. They wanted a change, but they needed to consider how changing the dress code would affect everyone. If students were allowed to wear anything, what would that mean for families who sent their children to the school because they valued a strict dress code? We couldn't make a decision until we had input from all voices, not just the loudest in the room.

As a student government we created a change management protocol, which walked any student with an idea through a step-by-step process to propose and gain approval by not only the student government but also the school administration. The first step was to give a detailed overview of proposed change, explain why the change is required, and describe the intended outcomes. The next step was to consider the potential benefits and adverse effects on all stakeholders, including the students, families, school staff, and larger community. The proposal was then presented to the student government and administration for approval. We created a practical guide to turn an idea into a lasting change.

It took a whole school year, but finally we are seeing changes in our school dress code. Now students can wear hoodies and a wider variety of shoes and pants. By creating these small changes, we gained hope that someday students can come to school and feel safe and comfortable in their skin. I'm proud that I was a part of this, and I'm even prouder that we created a system for change. We laid the foundation, and now the work continues.

Supporting a young person in achieving their goal for change certainly doesn't mean doing it for them. We want young people to grapple with real institutions, use real strategies, and interact with real people in power.

One high school student told me, "I don't want them to make student elections easy on me. I want to work for it. In just a few years, I'll be on my own. No one is going to hold my hand or pass me a ballot when they walk in the door. I want to practice figuring out where the polling station is and when the election will be held. I want to practice now, so I know what to do later." The more authentic we make experience like this, the more effective young people will be in making a difference.

Spark the Conversation

- If you could make any rule a law, what would it be?

- If you want to change something in your community who would support you? Who would oppose you?

- What are strategies you can use to convince others to make a change?

I heard someone say once, "Look for duct tape. Where there is duct tape, there is a problem to be solved." Have children hunt for duct tape with you, have them identify the problems, the pain points, the societal failures. Then leverage their curiosity to find a creative solution.

Young people have a perfect combination of a unique perspective and an altruistic imagination. Even their wildest ideas—eradicating homelessness, traveling to Pluto, becoming president, having recess all day long—are worth exploring. There are enough examples in this book alone to convince us that young people can accomplish amazing things.

Once you have helped a young person gather their wildly hopeful ideas, use your wisdom and knowledge of how the world works to help them with their efforts. Talk to them about the real dynamics of power and how to navigate actual institutions to create change. You might just visit them on Pluto one day.

8

Fearlessly Kind—
Elevating Kids' Values

> I wish people all around the world would be nice to others, what I mean by that is to not bully, not steal, not argue and treat others the way you want to be treated, that means if you helped someone or be nice to someone that person would do the same to you, also I hope that no one is not nice to someone and also to not push, shove, yell and complain, that is my wish.

In social studies one year, I was teaching my students about local government. We took a trip to Denver's gold-domed State Capitol and the Governor's Mansion. One little boy was enamored by the fact that if he were elected governor, he would get to live in this mansion. He declared his candidacy for governor one day and earned the nickname "El Gobernador" for the rest of the year.

For one lesson, I wanted my students to experience life as a mayor and asked them to create a mock city budget. I split the class into groups and gave each group a list of budget items. I included all the typical expenditures such as education, transportation, public safety, and sewers. I also threw in a few special projects like brand-new school playgrounds, high-tech libraries, and a new football stadium for the Denver Broncos.

Then I passed out tax revenue—plastic bags with $1 million bills photocopied on bright green paper. Of course, the amount of money was not enough to fund every single budget item. They would need to make hard choices. Soon there was a frenzy of arguments. At least one person in each group was shouting at their classmates. No one was listening to each other. I noticed one kid had grabbed a handful of bills and shoved them in his desk. This mock local government was getting a little too authentic.

I gathered the class together. I told the students they would have to make decisions based on their values. I wrote the words "I value _____, so I want to fund _____. What do you value?"

Then, I sent the kids back to their groups, and I was pleased to see that the tone of their conversation changed. They said things like, "I value playing, so I want to fund new playgrounds." Kids were able focus on their values as the basis for decision making, but they also practiced listening to the values of others.

While there was no right or wrong answer to the budgeting assignment, I wanted students to learn that values should drive decision making. It's a skill I want them to carry with them as adults.

I also remember their wide-eyed gasps when I closed the lesson by explaining that sometimes real grown-ups are unable to agree on a budget and sometimes end up shutting down part of the government.

MY WISH FOR THE WORLD

Naomi O'Brien, teacher and activist

So much of kindergarten is teaching students to be successful as students and as citizens. Like many teachers, I do, indeed, teach my kindergarteners to be kind, but in my classroom kindness doesn't start with sharing toys and end with taking turns on the slide. The kindness I want my students to learn is more nuanced, more robust. It is a kindness that is not always comfortable.

I want children to respect the playground rules and also respect the dignity of every person. I want them to be considerate with compliments and also consider how their choices impact others. I want children to be generous with gifts and also generous of spirit, of time, and of labor. My aim is for students to show kindness, not solely through schoolyard niceties, but also through an unrelenting desire for justice.

With this as my goal, I must speak to my students about struggle. I must explicitly teach about bigotry and hate. Yes, I talk to five-year-olds about racism and sexism. Even in kindergarten, we explore concepts of privilege, bias, and discrimination. Why? Because in the words of Dr. David Stovall, "If children are old enough to experience racism, they are old enough to talk about it."

(Continues)

(*MY WISH FOR THE WORLD, Naomi O'Brien Cont.*)

When February rolls around, I don't pass out work-sheets or have my students make crafts that feature a smiling cartoon of Rosa Parks or Martin Luther King Jr. No, I teach them the truth. Dr. King was an activist, a fighter. He worked tirelessly to ease the very real pain his community experienced and is still experiencing today. Coloring a romanticized version of Dr. King will not make my students more kind; acknowledging his struggle will. Discussing the fact that many people still face similar struggles helps my students begin to understand events that occur in our country on a daily basis. It can help them name what has happened to them, their friends, or their families. I don't perpetuate the myth that racism is over. When I have honest conversations with my students, I hope to inspire children who will grow up to be empathetic to the struggles that black men and women still face today as a direct result of this country's history.

When the fifth of May came around this year, I gathered my students together. We learned about the true history of Cinco de Mayo and about the Battle of Puebla and the victory of the Mexican army over their occupiers. We also talked about stereotypes. I showed them pictures from the Internet of other classrooms that were also celebrating Cinco de Mayo, but with worksheets, crafts, and activities laden with images of sombreros and tacos. I remember the confusion that crossed their faces. They audibly gasped. One boy asked me, "Why would people do that? It's a stereotype." I answered honestly, "Either they don't know that they are wrong or they know and don't care." "I care," shouted a few kids. We promised each other that if we saw anyone celebrating Cinco de Mayo with stereotypes, we would correct them and tell them the true history behind this holiday.

Empowering students, even our youngest students, to use their voices, to speak out, and to stand up for others—this is what makes children powerfully, fearlessly kind. It is not a happy addition to an education. It is the basis for an education. It is up to every educator, every mentor, and every caring adult to teach the true value of kindness.

I wish the world would honor children's ability to handle the truth and have big conversations, ideas, and feelings about injustice. I wish we could see that in doing this work we can all work collectively to raise a generation that can truly change the world.

I wish that no bad things would hapen in this world.

Guiding Values

I set my students on a mission. They needed to choose three guiding values that would drive our work during the school year. I started by giving students a list of about thirty values. I included some of universal values such as kindness, honesty, and gratitude. Then I listed some educational buzzwords: grit, collaboration, and rigor. I also listed values that are rarely publicly claimed but do indeed drive many of people's decisions: wealth, achievement, entertainment, and popularity.

Each of those values were written on little pieces of paper so kids could sort them into two initial groupings: "Very Important" and "Not So Important." From there we narrowed them down to the top twenty, then the top ten, then the top five. I assumed the next step would be to hold a simple vote for the final three values, but my students stopped me. Several kids wanted the chance to convince their peers to vote for their chosen value. Like most of my best lessons, I followed the students' lead.

I invited anyone one who wanted to campaign for a value up to the front of the room. It was one of the most heartwarming moments of my teaching career to watch my students passionately argue for the importance of values such as determination or learning. One girl said, "Guys, you have to vote for determination. What if you just give up? You won't be able to do anything!" A boy said, "Hello! We are at a school, we have to choose learning as a value. That's why we're here." After the speeches, we were ready for the final vote. I passed out sticky notes, and kids cast their vote, then I hustled the kids off to music class.

I tallied the votes. Honestly, I was surprised at the winners. They weren't the values I would have chosen, but in the end, the kids chose exactly the right ones: community, loyalty, and friendship.

When I thought about it, I realized each of the values my students chose—the values they wanted to drive their learning—were communal in nature. Loyalty, friendship, and community are values about how we all treat each other, how we interact and relate to each other. What a strong statement, especially if you consider the American education system's obsession with individual achievement.

Those three values became the axel that everything in our classroom rotated around. Each kid decorated a letter, and we hung up L-O-Y-A-L-T-Y, F-R-I-E-N-D-S-H-I-P, and C-O-M-M-U-N-I-T-Y in big, bright letters on the back wall of the classroom. When I sent kids off to work on assignments, I asked each one which value they were going to work on. We learned the sign for each value in American Sign Language and before students burst through the doors to recess, they signed the value they would show while playing outside.

One day, a math lesson completely fell apart. Students were supposed to be working in partners, but I looked up and saw that not one single kid was working. The lesson was a disaster. Even the kids I could usually count on to be focused and diligent students were goofing around. After a round of reminders and stern warnings had not helped the situation at all, I called all the kids to come together on our classroom rug.

At the top of a large, white sheet of poster paper, I wrote "What Our Values Look Like in Math." I divided the poster into three sections labeled loyalty, friendship, and community. Kids helped me fill in each section. They told me that in math loyalty is helping someone understand how to solve a problem, friendship is making sure your friend knows what to do, and community is concentrating and working hard so everyone in class has a chance to focus and learn. There was so much power in having children take a moment and reflect on a simple question: Are you living your values?

Initially, I thought I was the driving force behind these values. After all, I was the one who set up all the voting, and it was me who kept referencing the values during our lessons. But on Valentine's Day I realized my students were just as invested in the guiding values as I was. One girl brought in a shoebox to collect Valentines, and it caught my eye. Inside of a heart, a little girl had written the words "loyalty, friendship, community." The values were so much a part of our class that she used them as decoration. When the school bell rang another morning, a boy came up to me and showed me his black T-shirt. "Do you know why I wore this shirt today?" he asked. He pointed to neon-yellow letters that spelled loyalty.

Upon reflection, I think 100 percent of the power of our guiding values came from the students. It's not about getting kids to buy in to my agenda. It's about elevating the values my students already have. Children need to be given the opportunity to name, define, and live out their own values.

The Value of a Name

Many people do not think of Colorado as stronghold of the Ku Klux Klan. Yet, at one point in Colorado's history it had the second highest per capita Klan membership of any state. In the 1920s, Colorado's governing bodies were controlled by the KKK. A *New York Times* article explained, "By 1924, the Klan had won control of the mayor's office, the city police, the governor's seat, both United States Senate seats, and much of the state legislature. Hooded men marched through Denver; opponents were kidnapped and pistol-whipped."

Many influential people in Colorado's history were associated with the KKK, but "The peak of the Klan's influence in many ways was the embrace of Denver Mayor Ben Stapleton of the Klan's ideology," as Terrance Carroll, former Colorado Speaker of the House explained in a PBS documentary.

That name Stapleton is well known in Denver. Benjamin Stapleton held the mayor's office for twenty years. The airport was named after him. When the airport closed and the land redeveloped, the surrounding neighborhood kept his name. Now, multiple businesses, organizations, and schools bare the name of a former mayor who was also a registered Klansman.

Should a neighborhood and the schools inside it be named after a Klansman? The question was raised by community organizers with Black Lives Matter in 2015 and has sparked debate ever since. As a response to the public dialogue, writing teacher P. J. Shields partnered with fellow teachers BreOnna Tindall and Chrissy Schulz to create a research project in which every student at Denver School of Science and Technology Stapleton Middle School would learn about the school's namesake.

After reading historical documents, debating ideas in Socratic seminars, holding schoolwide meetings, and writing essays about Ben Stapleton, the students took a survey. When the results were tallied, 58 percent of students believed the name should change, 12 percent were unsure, and 30 percent preferred to keep the name. A group of students presented their positions to school leadership who agreed to consider the issue.

This project clearly impacted students. In a story reported by Colorado Public Radio, seventh-grader Brooklyn Luckett, who is African American, shared her views. When asked what she thought of the school name, she responded, "I kind of felt unsure about my safety, about what my school was about 'cause our core values were, responsibility, respect, integrity, courage, and doing your best. After I read a couple articles and learned some more background about him, it revealed to me that he didn't live what our school is supposed to embody."

Shields was not surprised when students like Brooklyn brought up the school values, saying, "Our school's core values are integrated into every school day. Students become very familiar with them. It's natural that they would leverage the core values in understanding this issue."

While many students used the school's core values as guide-posts, they did not perceive the values in exactly the same way. Shields told me that many students brought up the value of integrity. They did not believe Stapleton showed this value, and as such he should not be honored with a school name. Shields also told me that one student cited the value of respect. He believed Ben Stapleton was an influential and accomplished historical figure. It would be disrespectful to remove his name.

Through this project, Shields and fellow teachers gave students the opportunity to articulate opinions informed both by academic research and their own lived experience. These teachers did what all caring adults should do. They gave young people the space to interpret and define their own values as well as help young people apply those values to their world. As caring adults, if we present values to young people, we must be prepared to live up to those values.

After much advocacy by students, the school leadership has agreed to change the name. As of early 2019, leaders and students are working to select a name that reflects the values of the entire school community.

Try This . . .

BUNDLE CHALLENGES
TO FIND SOLUTIONS

Sometimes, people are even more motivated to help others than to help themselves. The United Nations International Childrens Emergency Fund (UNICEF) recognized this and came up with an elegant solution that addresses two seemingly opposite challenges at the same time. They knew many children need opportunities to become more active, while at the same time many children around the world are malnourished. By bundling these two challenges, they created an ingenious program called UNICEF Kid Power.

UNICEF Kid Power gives kids the power to save lives by connecting their everyday activity to real-world impact. When kids get active with UNICEF Kid Power, they "unlock" impact. For example, if they do UNICEF Kid Power Ups, which are free brain breaks that get kids moving, they earn lifesaving nutrition packets that UNICEF delivers to children suffering from severe, acute malnutrition. My students love doing Kid Power Ups— the more they move, the more lives they help save! To date, UNICEF Kid Power has distributed 11.3 million Ready-to-Use Therapeutic Food (RUTF) packets. This means kids across the United States have helped save nearly eighty thousand severely malnourished children around the world!

(Continues)

(TRY THIS, Bundle Challenges to Find Solutions Cont.)

Even better, the program offers free educational re-sources that help students learn about the world around them, become aware and engaged, and develop critical twenty-first-century skills that empower them to work to-gether and solve everyday challenges. When students complete UNICEF Kid Power activities, they earn Kid Power Points, which is like a digital currency. Through the UNICEF Kid Power Exchange, classrooms can then direct their points to support the causes that matter most to them, such as local animal shelters or food drives.

From what I have seen, this bundling of challenges, such as malnutrition and the need to move more, has been very effective in my classroom. The values of generosity, sharing, and helping are deeply ingrained in children and serve as motivation. Caring adults can maximize young people's efforts by bundling challenges.

For example, my school hosts a canned food drive ev-ery year in order to address food insecurity in our commu-nity. We also have issues with chronic absenteeism. We could bundle these issues and allow classrooms that met their attendance goals to decide which food pantry or shelter to donate the canned food to. Students would be motivated to increase their attendance by helping others.

There is an opportunity to reimagine the rewards used to motivate young people. I remember when I was a child, my softball coach said, "If we win this game, I'll take you all out for ice cream." What if we change this motivational strategy slightly? Instead of earning a treat for themselves, players could earn an ice cream party for patients at a children's hospital. Likewise, instead of earning a prize at the spelling bee, the winner could choose five books to donate to the library. Or perhaps for every ticket sold to the school play, the actors will pledge one minute of time teaching acting workshops to younger kids. With a little nudge from adults, I'm sure kids would come up with creative, impactful bundles.

We can leverage the values young people hold to motivate them. In doing so, we may be able to address multiple challenges at the same time and more importantly empower young people to use their efforts to make a difference.

I wish the world was more peacefull. If you flip on the news at almost any moment you will see hate, crime, war, racism, and shootings.

Spark the Conversation

- What are your values?

- Who do you admire for holding strong values?

- Have you ever been in a situation where it was difficult to live out your values?

- Are there values that are universal?

When talking to a young person about values, allow them to direct the conversation. They hear enough messages from adults about how they should act and how they should treat people. Give them the space to express their own values to you.

When conflict arises in their life, invite them to explore it from the lens of values. When kids fight in my class, one question I ask them is simply, "How do you think people in this class should be treated?" It's a good starting point to resolving conflict because kids usually say that everyone in the class should be respected, treated fairly, and given second chances. From there, you can help a child verbalize what they value and how those values should show up in their actions.

9

Give Children Choices

> I wish that adolts wold treat me serios.

There were traffic cones in the middle of the rug to represent the Rocky Mountains, boxes on the side for Colorado's Western Plateau, flipped-over bowls to form the shape of hills, and four strategically placed jumpropes to make up the major rivers. It's fair to say our classroom was a mess, but we had created a giant 3D map of Colorado's geography. My students were grasping Colorado's landforms, but I wanted to take their learning further.

I sent home a note. My instructions were simple: "Make a map of Colorado. There are no rules. Be creative." I figured the kids would produce some fun maps, but I did not expect that they would be so . . . delicious. One girl brought in a sheet cake with blue frosting for rivers and purple fondant mountain peaks. One boy used Microsoft paint to make a digital map of Colorado. Other kids drew pictures, and some kids made posters. A few kids created dioramas with miniature trees in the mountains and cars in the cities. The students all became experts on Colorado geography because they were able to chase their own learning down a path of their own choosing.

I WISH... I Could teach art to little People. I Could teach people art so I Can teach the Basics and be creative.

When Children Have Choice

When I was in college, my friends and I reveled in the first week of a new term. We called it "syllabus week." The only academic expectation of us was to show up and receive the syllabus. It was a like a collegiate staycation.

All of those syllabi read like a laundry list of choices I didn't have. Just like the ones I receive for every course since the seventh grade, the syllabus told me exactly what pages to read, exactly what papers to write, and exactly when those papers would be turned in. All decisions were made before I walked in the door.

My professors were the experts. They had studied and earned the degrees and abbreviations after their names. They were completely in charge of what I would learn. I did learn, but I learned the same things in the same exact way as everyone else. It didn't matter what students brought to class in terms of experience, curiosity, interest, or passion. There was one predetermined schedule of learning—the one listed on the back page of the syllabus.

This style of instruction is efficient and predictable. But maybe there is a better way. Imagine the power of a teacher's or professor's syllabus saying, "I'm an expert on this subject matter. I have devoted decades of my life to the study of this. What do *you* want to know about *my* expertise? How can *my* knowledge relate to *your* world?" It would be radical. It would be powerful.

But most adults don't ask those questions. Most of us are afraid of what will happen if we relinquish control. If we allow young people to have choices, they might choose wrong. They might fail. We want to protect young people from ambiguous threats, but that often robs young people of the benefits of choice. Choice is powerful, and young people should be taught how to wield that power.

Academically, choice has measurable impact on learning. Author of the book *Learning through Academic Choice*, Paula Denton explains, "When students have choices in their learning, they become highly engaged and productive. They're excited about learning and sharing their knowledge. They're likely to think more deeply and creatively, work with more persistence, and use a range of academic skills and strategies."

I saw this so clearly when I gave my students choice in creating their own maps of Colorado. Each map reflected the same geographic markers, but none looked the same. Instead, each map demonstrated the student's individual talents and interests. It would have been easier to assign the same exact project to everyone, but it would not have given my students the same depth of learning.

Of course, adults have more life experience and a wider breadth of scholastic knowledge than children. It's easier and more efficient for adults to make all the decisions. However, when we give children the opportunity to make choices in a supportive environment, they are more eager to do challenging work, more able to employ problem-solving strategies, and, most importantly, they become empowered. As caring adults, we must honor a young person's need for self-determination and embrace the benefits that come with allowing them to make their own choices.

Try This . . .

YOUR CHOICES, MY CHOICES

"You have some choices, and I have some choices." When I was student teaching, a veteran teacher said this, and I've used it ever since. It helps me ensure that I am including some level of choice in aspects of students' daily work. I typically say this when I am finishing a lesson and sending students off to complete classwork. It sounds something like this:

"You have choices, and I have choices. My choice is to have you work in partners to finish these math problems. Your choices are where you sit and which strategies you use."

You have choices, and I have choices. My choice is that we are writing about character traits. Your choice is which character you write about."

CHOICES TO CONSIDER:

LOCATION: Allow young people to self-select where they work or spend time. Just like adults, some children prefer to work in quiet spaces, while others prefer a more vibrant, exciting atmosphere. Some kids prefer to work at a desk, some kids prefer to sit on the floor, and some kids prefer to cuddle up in a little nook. I have also taught students who are sensitive to lighting. They work better with dim lighting, so allowing them to choose where they work makes them more comfortable and efficient.

ORDER: Allow young people to decide which order they'll complete tasks. Often, they will select tasks that they enjoy to do first. Completing those tasks will build momentum and help them finish less-appealing tasks. It also gives students practice in prioritizing their work.

NOW OR LATER: Whenever I ask a child to do something I know they don't want to do, I give them a simple option: now or later. "You have to take this test. Do you want to do it now or later?" Given those two choices, kids almost always choose later. That is perfectly fine with me. "Later" might come tomorrow, next week, or it might come in five minutes. Kids feel better about a task when they have a say in when it happens.

(Continues)

(TRY THIS, Your Choices, My Choices Cont.)

SKIP IT: When I am sending kids to work on an assign-ment, I will usually add, "Choose one question to skip." That little directive changes the way students approach their work. Kids feel like they have won a little prize. But as a teacher, I know there is no measurable effect on a student's learning to solve thirteen multiplication problems rather than fourteen. Instead, it forces kids to think criti-cally and evaluate the difficulty level of the questions. I can also see which problems or tasks kids skip. If most of the class avoids a certain type of question, I know that is an area to focus on in future lessons.

Real Kids Making Real Choices

Real readers make choices. They choose the literature they read and the media they consume. They decide where, when, and for how long they read. Choice is such a major element in any adult's reading habits. Yet, when it comes to young people, choice is not often considered an important literacy skill.

Just as I teach my students phonics and character develop-ment, I also teach my students to build their choice-making skills. On one of the first days of school, I start by putting several tubs of books on our classroom rug. I specifically pull a wide variety of books from different genres, topics, and difficulty levels. Then I have students go book shopping. I ask them to select books they want to read, and I also ask them to make a pile of books they would not choose. It's a first step in growing my students' ability to make good decisions as a reader.

Research has shown that the amount of choices readers have makes a difference. Michal Maimaran of the Kellogg School of Management at Northwestern University knew from previous research that "having lots of choices can feel overwhelming or make us regretful of our final choice—a phenomenon known as 'choice overload.'" She wanted to find out if this was true for children too.

In her study, preschoolers were tasked with choosing a book from a set. Some children were allowed to choose a book from a set of two, while others were given a set of seven books to choose from. Her results showed that choosing from the smaller set was indeed easier and more efficient. She found, "When kids pick from a large set of options, they spend less time engaged with their choice than when they pick from a small set."

However, her results show that choice is multifaceted. Almost all the children said they *preferred* to pick from the larger set. "The consensus was that the small set would make choosing easier, but choosing from a large set would be more fun." If our goal is to have children enjoy the process of reading, they should be allowed more options. I have seen the power of teaching my students the skills to self-select books, but I have also seen the damage caused when I attempt to control their choices too closely.

In education we have an obsession with "leveling" books. Some books are obviously harder to read than others, so through rubrics and algorithms educators developed systems to assign each book a level. One of the most popular leveling systems was created by professors Irene Fountas and Gay Su Pinnell. It ranks books from easiest, level A, to hardest, level Z. The letter, or level of difficulty, a child can read independently becomes their reading level.

Most literacy teachers see children progress quickly when they read at or slightly above their reading level. With that in mind, classrooms and libraries across the country have labeled books with levels in the hopes of building literacy skills quickly. As a new teacher, I was no different. I methodically organized my library by level. Every single book had a color-coded sticker on the covers with a level. I evaluated each of my students' reading ability and told them the specific bins of books that matched their reading level they were allowed to select from. At times—believe me I say this with shame—I would even go through a child's book selection and remove the books I deemed too easy or too hard for them. I felt the tighter my leash was on their book selection, the better readers they would become.

As I grew in experience as a teacher, I realized just how wrong I was. By so tightly controlling my students' reading, I was limiting their ability to select and enjoy books. The truth is, when a reader opens a book, they bring much more than phonics ability; they bring prior knowledge, personal experience, interest, and curiosity. Often, they bring a social motivation to read books their friends are reading. All of these aspects impact their ability to read and understand a text.

The irony is the creators of this leveling system themselves, Fountas and Pinnell, now realize how it has been implemented and have begun to push back. "We have never recommended that the school libraries or classroom libraries be leveled or that levels be reported to parents. We want students to learn to select books the way experienced readers do—according to their own interests, by trying a bit of the book, by noticing the topic or the author."

Now, instead of limiting choice, I leverage it. I don't ban books anymore and instead use the term "power book." I explain this is a book that will push them to be a better reader because it is slightly challenging but not overwhelmingly difficult. I encourage students to spend most of their independent reading time with a power book that is right in their literacy sweet spot, but I empower my students to make choices for themselves. Guide choice, don't control it.

Guidelines for Choice

If we want to ensure choice and all its benefits are present in young people's lives, it's helpful to have some guidelines.

First and foremost, there are times when adults need to withhold the ability to choose. Obviously, a child should not be allowed to make a choice that will harm them. With my students, I use the term "zero choice."

One year we visited the Denver Art Museum for a field trip. After eating lunch, we had a few spare minutes so we decided to swing by Denver's State Capitol building a few blocks away. During that walk, my students had very limited choices. They had to be in two lines between adults. I told them, "This is a zero choice time. You have to be on the sidewalk between the adult chaperones. Cars are moving fast, and if you step into the crosswalk early you might get hit." It's important to note that, even though I heavily controlled my students' behavior at that moment, I was explicit about my expectations, and I offered an explanation. I wanted them to know what to do, and I also wanted them to know why.

So often, adults say, "Stop!" "Don't!" "Not now!" We are often acting in the best interest of the child. We want to keep them safe. The problem is, if we only say, "Don't!" we are missing out on an opportunity to teach them why. Young children need to connect our commands with reasons. That is how they learn to make safe choices. So when children have zero choices, it is incumbent on us to make sure they know why.

With the exception being made for clear and present danger, most of the time it is appropriate to ensure young people have access to choice. How we offer that choice makes a difference.

In their scholarly review titled *When Choice Motivates and When It Does Not*, Idit Katz and Avi Assor lay out three aspects of choice based on self-determination theory. When ensuring choice, we should call to mind autonomy, competence, and relatedness.

First, autonomy refers to having control over your life. It's not just being allowed to choose by yourself; it's being allowed to choose something of significance to you. Katz and Assor explain, "Feelings of autonomy are particularly strong when the task is perceived as being closely connected to the values, interests, and goals that constitute the core of one's authentic self and identity." If we are allowing young people to choose, but not connecting their decision to a higher level of interest, it's not really choosing, it's just picking.

Second, we all have a desire to feel successful. This is the human need for competence. It is the ability to effectively deal with our environment. We want to make choices that make us feel competent. When choice-making is too complex, we use less-effective strategies. Choices that overwhelmed us with stress or self-doubt are not motivating, but neither are easy choices. When given an option, most people don't choose easy or hard tasks, instead they self-select intermediate-level choices so they can feel challenged and demonstrate their abilities.

Finally, feeling connected to others can impact our choices. It is our need for relatedness that drives us both to care for others and also to be cared for. We want our choices to matter to others.

So we should help young people see how their choices affect others.

All in all, choice does motivate, but it has to be the right choice. Katz and Assor explain, "In order for choice to be motivating, it has to be based on a careful match between the various options and the students' needs, interests, goals, abilities, and cultural background."

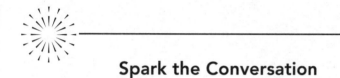

Spark the Conversation

- What choices do you make every day?

- Have you ever made a difficult choice? What strategies did you use to make that decision?

- What areas of your life do you wish you had the power to make more choices?

We want children to make good choices, but we often neglect to provide enough practice with choice-making. If you are like me, then you want to provide children with as much opportunity as possible to make choices in a supportive and forgiving environment. To find out when this can happen, we can simply ask. Children are acutely aware of what is decided *by* them and what is decided *for* them. They can help you identify areas where there is an opportunity to provide more choice

We can also talk to young people about what makes a choice difficult. Literature can be a great outlet for these discussions. My students read a book where the character has to decide between helping their family and helping their friend. We talked about the idea of competing motivations. We had a rich conversation about how there are circumstance when the right choice is not obvious. Talk through difficult choices with kids, and help them see the possible outcomes of their decisions.

10

Hearing Every Voice

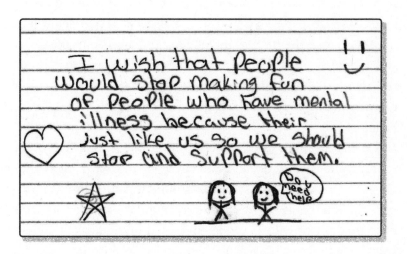

It's shocking but true that young people are often not even considered experts in their own lives. We adults do so much in the interest of improving the lives of young people: we build parks, operate youth sports leagues, and run school systems all for the benefit of young people. Yet, we rarely see young people as stakeholders in the systems we created for them. At times we might seek input from young people, but do we truly share in decision making? Do we allow young people the opportunity to be heard? Do we reap the benefits of youth voices?

There is so much to be gained when we hear all voices. "The evidence is pretty clear that when organizations, including schools, give young people agency and voice, and integrate their perspectives into decision-making processes, those organizations are more effective in the work they're trying to do," says Gretchen Brion-Meisels, of the Harvard Graduate School of Education.

We adults just get caught up in the daily demands of our work. As a teacher, I know this pitfall well. It can seem like a burden to take the time to include another person in the discussion when we already have so much to do. However, listening to the thoughts and opinions of young people is not just doing them a favor. They have insight and perspective that we can benefit from.

I often have my students weigh in on the layout of my classroom. Whenever I do, kids are overflowing with ideas. Even though I have had the same classroom and furniture for years, my students come up with new configurations I never would have thought of before. Once, they used high and low tables to create stadium-style seating behind my classroom rug. They moved a shelf of cubbies so that it was easier to get their breakfast each morning. My favorite student idea was when my students moved around kid-sized sofas in order to make a cozy reading nook.

My students become co-creators of their classroom. They develop a sense of ownership over the space, which causes students to take a more active role in keeping the classroom clean and organized. More than that, my students came up with better ideas than I did. If I had never involved my students in the design of my classroom, it wouldn't be the inviting, imaginative space it is today. This is exactly what Brion-Meisels means when she says, "Listening to young people doesn't mean unilaterally considering their perspective; it means recognizing that young people have a perspective on the world that adults can't share, and that their perspective should be welcomed alongside the wisdom adult perspectives bring."

I wish to make an impact on poverty by donating to charity or creating a charity that donates its money to people living in poverty.

MY POWER

Ahmed Eltayeb,
sixteen-year-old student

I was open, but skeptical. Mr. Tommer, the dean of my high school and one of the few African Americans on staff, had encouraged me to join a new group called Colorado Youth Congress. He said I could learn leadership skills. While I wasn't completely sold, I was willing to give it a shot.

At the first meeting, I learned we would be working on civic change projects. In teams, we would spend one year working across lines of race, class, and politics to lead systemic change on a chosen issue. We divided into groups and sat facing each other in a circle of chairs. An adult facilitated and asked us two questions: What frustrates you most about your school, city, country, or world? And what do you think is possible for our future?

Soon, it was my turn, and I told the group my story. My parents had moved here from Sudan, chasing the American Dream, and built a good life for my two brothers and me. For my family, education is a top priority. I enjoyed school, but when I went to class there was a nagging feeling of resignation I couldn't quite shake. I felt like my voice didn't matter.

It wasn't always that way. My elementary school, just like my neighborhood, was full of families from all over the world. It was effortless back then. Regardless of our race, all the kids played together at recess, and we sat with each other at lunch. The school even hosted a world culture day where we celebrated holidays from around the world. I remember they had everything translated in English, Spanish, and Arabic for our families.

Something changed when I began attending middle school farther away from home. While there is a good amount of student diversity in my new middle and high school, the neighborhood the school is in is mostly white and affluent. In school, we talk about inclusion a lot, but the truth is when you walk into the cafeteria, you see most of the white kids sitting together in one corner, most of the Latinx students together in another, and most of the African American students eating together, too. There is a tension I have never been comfortable with.

That tension silenced me. I tried to speak out and share ideas for how to improve the school, but nothing substantial came of it. Once, other Muslim students and I gave a presentation to the whole school about Eid-al-Fitr, an important holiday in my faith. That same day, another student said, "It's funny that Muslims are peaceful during the month of Eid, but the other eleven months they are terrorists." I felt defeated.

I wanted to be heard, not just allowed to speak. When I was sharing that with the group at Colorado Youth Congress, I realized I wasn't alone. So many of us felt voiceless. We decided to use that common theme—that shared point of frustration—to drive our work. Together, we would find a way to have our voices heard.

(Continues)

(*MY POWER, Ahmed Eltayeb Cont.*)

We brainstormed several solutions and realized it was the school board that controlled much of our education. Yet, the school board was not actually accountable to us, the students. Instead they were accountable to the voters. In order for our voices to be heard, our votes had to count. Our goal was to grant sixteen- and seventeen-year-olds the right to vote for their representative on the school board in official elections.

When my team and I started researching, we realized our goal was not as radical as we had thought. Several localities in Maryland and California had already done it. Closer to home, we found out there were local organizations that had been engaged in this work for years. Finding allies motivated us, but we realized we needed a champion in the legislature. We found that when we were introduced to State Representative James Coleman.

Representative Coleman heard our case and believed in the cause. He helped us organize a student lobbying day. Months of work culminated in thirty students, including myself, spending the day at the State Capitol. We provided lawmakers with research, showing that people who start voting at age sixteen are more likely to vote in the future. There is even evidence of a trickle-up effect of parents voting at higher rates when their children vote. We presented data about the cost of enfranchising sixteen- and seventeen-year-olds and answered their questions. Most importantly, we told our personal stories and shared what having a voice in the school board would mean to us.

We have made progress, but our work is not done yet. Moving forward, we plan to build public support by connecting with statewide stakeholders and organizing more youth. We haven't won the vote yet, but I finally feel like I have a voice.

I use my power to lift up the stories of others. We all have a voice, and it's my mission to make that voice count.

Why Choice?

In my sophomore year of college, I took an English course with a focus on democracy. On the last day of class our professor surprised us with one final assignment. As students, we had to determine our own grades. But we had to make a decision as a group, democratically.

This was not a hypothetical activity or a thought experiment. The students, not the professor, had to decide how much each test, homework assignment, essay, and class participation was "worth" in terms of our grade.

The simplest strategy would have been to weigh each component equally so that our grades for tests, homework, essays, and class participation each counted for 25 percent of our overall grade. The problem was that each student was looking out for their own self-interest. The students who missed class a lot proposed to make class participation worth 0 percent of the final grade. Students who aced the tests wanted the tests to be worth 100 percent. At first, we all wanted to rig the grading formula to benefit us personally.

It didn't take long for us to find a more logical method. Someone thought class participation should be worth more because it demonstrated effort. I thought, altruistically, there must be some solution that would allow us all to walk away with As, but the numbers just didn't work out. Proposals that benefited some inevitably hurt others. At one point, I figured we all would be stuck in that room until nightfall.

In the end, one student came up with a pragmatic approach. She asked each student individually which grade we thought we deserved. I thought I should earn an A. I worked hard, learned the material, and never missed a class or assignment. Surprisingly, that attitude was not shared by all. Several students who seemed to missed class sporadically said they would accept a B, and the others who put in average effort were fine with getting a C. So, she proposed a relatively simple plan where tests and essays were heavily weighted, and we each calculated what that would mean for our individual grades. We tweaked the plan until it yielded the acceptable grades for everyone. Somehow we all came to consensus and walked away satisfied. It was an ideal, if not rare, outcome for any democracy.

This final lesson was a powerful one. The exercise brought the philosophies and ideologies we had studied all semester to life by democratizing the classroom. For the first time, the students had real decision-making power over something as important as our official grades.

Looking back, I wonder why that level of student voice and decision making was such a rare experience. The original catalyst for creating free and public education system was to produce an informed citizenry to participate in our democracy. Yet, ironically, schools as a whole are terrified of allowing students to participate democratically in their own education. Shelley Berman with Educators for Social Responsibility once said, "We teach reading, writing, and math by [having students do] them, but we teach democracy by lecture."

As college students, almost all of us had the right to vote for our government, but we rarely had any such voice in our own classes. We adults should take a more active role in harnessing the power of voice for the young people in our lives. As former principal Nelson Beaudoin said, "I have come to trust student voice as a powerful tool for school improvement, a liberating force for student engagement, and a crucial element in educating for participatory democracy."

Nothing About Us Without Us

When Candi DiBeca returned to school after summer break as a sophomore, something unexpected happened to her high school. The school district decided to restructure the school, breaking it into three smaller separate high schools and stretching already scarce resources of the 100 percent free and reduced lunch student body in a predominantly African American and Latinx neighborhood. Electives and honor classes were eliminated in favor of experimental curriculum. "I felt like we became the guinea pigs of the school district," explained Candi. The school district made all of these decisions without involving students or the broader community.

Four years later, a sophomore in college this time, Candi heard about an even more drastic change. The restructuring had failed

Try This . . .

SPECTRUM OF ENGAGEMENT

The International Association for Public Participation is a non-profit organization with the goal of promoting public engagement in institutions and governments. It created the Spectrum of Public Participation, which can be adapted to become a helpful tool to clarify the role that young people have in our decision-making processes.

There five levels of engagement: inform, consult, involve, collaborate, and empower.

Inform	Adults will keep young people informed.
Consult	Adults will listen to and acknowledge the concerns and aspirations of young people.
Involve	Adults will work with young people to ensure their concerns and aspirations are directly reflected in decisions.
Collaborate	Adults will look to young people for advice and innovation in formulating solutions and incorporate that advice and recommendations into the decisions.
Empower	Adults will implement what young people decide.

Source: Adapted from IAP2's Spectrum of Public Participation.

These are levels and not sequential steps. One level is not inherently better than another. Rather, each level has a different purpose and should be used to serve different needs. For example, a soccer coach might just *inform* her team that practice is canceled because of snow. When it comes to calling plays during a game, that coach might *collaborate* with players to combine her expertise with the players' experience on the field. That same coach might *empower* players to design and order the uniforms.

Young people need the opportunity to participate in decision making at each of these levels, yet typically we they are only permitted to inform and consult. To combat this, make a list of all the decisions that are made in your organization. Then categorize each decision with the level of engagement young people can expect. Ask yourself, which of these can become opportunities for young people to engage at higher levels?

at her old school, enrollment was down, and the school district had now decided to close down her high school. Once again, the community was not engaged in decision making.

"As a student, as a community member, I felt I had no voice in the process. None of us did. I couldn't remain silent any longer while students in my community weren't receiving a quality education," Candi explained to me. She set about creating an organization called Project VOYCE, which stands for Voices of Youth Changing Education. Every year, a cohort of underrepresented youth ages 14 to 25 are trained to identify and address root causes of inequity in their own communities. Once trained, the young people speak at conferences, help draft education policy, testify to the legislature, and partner with schools to promote student engagement and political activism.

One middle school brought in Project VOYCE to help solve a problem that had dumbfounded the administration and teachers for years. Many students clearly had strong academic abilities, but they were not showing up or passing their classes. The teachers referred to these students as the "can-but-won't kids."

The young people trained by Project VOYCE recruited students from that middle school. The middle school students were taught how to conduct Youth Participatory Action Research (YPAR) and identify the cause of the problem at their own school. Through focus groups, interviews, and surveys, the problem became incredibly clear. Every mode of data collected pointed to the same thing: the students did not feel respected by their teachers. "Honestly, a lack of respect has been a major theme in our work," said Candi, "Young people often feel devalued by adults. When young people don't feel respected, they disengage. We have found that academic outcomes and engagement improve when adults shift their energy toward showing young people respect."

Based on their findings, the students made three key recommendations to their own middle school. First, students and teachers should begin with co-creating a shared definition of respect. The middle school teachers seemed to interpret respect as a version of compliance, but the students saw things differently. One student found it disrespectful that students were not allowed to eat in class, but the teacher always ate her lunch during lessons. Others students felt disrespected when teachers did not put effort into building relationships with them. Clarifying what respect looks like to all parties as well as building cross-cultural understanding among students and teachers who frequently looked different and had a much different upbringing was crucial to changing the climate of the school.

Second, the middle school students recommended that teachers utilize "Fast, Frequent Feedback" protocols. Students wanted an opportunity to weigh in on what was working in their classes. They wanted an open dialogue, not just about the content of their courses, but also about how they felt in class.

Third, the students urged teachers to provide more instructional choices. One-size-fits-all assignments had taken a toll on students' motivation. They wanted to demonstrate their knowledge in ways that were meaningful to them, like teaching their peers, creating videos, presenting speeches, or writing songs. When students had the freedom to express their learning in a way they chose, they would be more motivated to learn.

Everyone—the administration, teachers, and students—were all present in the same school every day. They were among each other, but they weren't having the same experience nor were they truly engaging with each other. They did not consider each other partners in learning.

The work that groups such as Project VOYCE have done teaches us that adults can work more effectively with youth when there is true partnership. Youth collaborate more when they feel their intelligence is valued, when their potential for growth is taken into account, when they are allowed to make choices and discoveries, and when they feel safe. As Candi explained, "When young people are empowered to use *their* voices and define terms of engagement, they improve systems for everyone, not just themselves."

I wish I could change the world by changing the immigration laws and the seperation of families at the border. The reasons why I would want to change these problems are because most of them in my opinion are somewhat harsh. To me it does not seem fair that a 4 year old has to be separated from his mother just because she was born in a different country. I could change these laws by advocating

---

✦

MY WISH FOR THE WORLD

Desmond Williams,
educator

It was my fourth year teaching at a small, independent all-boys school in an underserved community of Washington, DC. When I met my new class, I had an uneasy feeling that student voice had being stifled. There was only one class per grade level, which meant that after several years together the third-grade students in my classroom were adept at getting on each other's nerves. Everyone knew everyone, which was great most of the time but at other times presented challenges.

One student in particular was treated as an oddity. Zion had an attorney's vocabulary at the age of eight. He rarely finished reading an entire book because his love of words would sidetrack him. He kept a journal to record newly discovered words. There were at least ninety words in it before October. Zion was not interested in the typical pursuits of the other young boys. While the rest of my boys obsessed over football, spinning Beyblades, or talking about all things wrestling, Zion kept to himself, accompanied by what he loved most, comic books.

Zion drew and drew. He created his own superheroes and complete worlds for them to exist in. This had earned him the ridicule of his classmates. Consumed by his own world, Zion often agitated his previous teacher, and she would take her frustrations out on the entire class, who in turn would take it out on Zion. That was the Zion I was introduced to, considered an annoyance to his peers and finding escape in his own imagination.

One day, instead of cleaning up for recess, Zion was doodling his latest creation, I-man, a superhero with the power of invisibility. I walked over and picked up the drawing.

"Just throw it away, Mr. Williams," hollered one student.

"Here we go again; you're always drawing that stupid junk," said another.

"I can't stand him," came from someone in the back.

I brushed off their remarks. Trashing his comic was never an option; I have a strict rule of never throwing away a child's creation, even if it is just a doodle. Even if it was prolonging lining up for recess.

(Continues)

(MY WISH FOR THE WORLD, Desmond Williams Cont.)

It was only November, but it was clear that my class had a habit of piling on Zion and silencing him. I wouldn't allow that to continue. I had to find a way to empower Zion and help him find his voice.

I told Zion, loudly enough for the rest of the boys to hear, "I was just like you! I got in trouble all the time for drawing in class. Make sure to grab your drawing off my desk at the end of the day. It's really good." I wanted to make sure the class knew I accepted and identified with Zion.

In a series of morning meetings, I made it my goal to send an important message to the entire class. We all have gifts and talents. We all have a voice and something to contribute. I led discussions in which we talked about what made us unique, including our hobbies and our interests. I took care to emphasize that all passions were equal. I stressed that students passionate about football are not more relevant or cooler than the child who was passionate about soccer. Likewise, the kid interested in soccer is no more relevant than the kid who likes to bake or read or even create comic books.

My final strategy to empower Zion and solidify equal voice for my entire class was to initiate genius hour. Every Wednesday, children got to spend the last hour of the school day working on a "genius project." The boys could choose any academic interest or creative pursuit that they were passionate about. The chief stipulation was all projects had to be completely unrelated to what we were studying in our lessons. I still regard genius hour as one of the smartest decisions I ever made as a classroom teacher.

Zion spent his genius hour fleshing out his I-man character, but he did not have to hide or feel ashamed. In fact, his classmates became co-conspirators in rounding out I-man's superpowers. They helped create I-man's arch-enemy and co-wrote some his adventures.

It became clear that Zion was fully embraced by his classmates and the larger school community. His classmates began to appreciate him for his verbal acumen as well. As Zion got older, he became the go-to emcee for schoolwide assemblies and community gatherings.

While I knew there had been a shift in how Zion was received by his peers, I did not expect what happened when Zion was in fifth grade. Our boys were about to receive an epic surprise: free tickets to the movie *Black Panther*, and the local news was coming to our school to film the story. The reporter only wanted to interview one student, so we let the boys choose who it would be.

Zion's classmates unanimously chose him. The interests and passions that had once ostracized him, his highly developed vocabulary, and his love of comic books made Zion the most qualified. When asked what seeing *Black Panther* meant to him, the boy who had once created a whole world for an invisible man and had now been chosen to be the voice for his peers, responded, "He is just symbolizing black power."

I wish the world would embrace all voices.

Spark the Conversation

- When do you feel heard?

- How can you share your thoughts and opinions with people in power?

- Is there something I could do to make sure I listen to your ideas better?

Being allowed to speak and being heard are two very different things. Many young people struggle not only to communicate their ideas effectively but also to find a receptive audience. When a young person feels like they are not being heard, we need to validate that experience and drill down deeper to find out more.

Maybe that young person is waiting for an invitation to share their thoughts and opinions. Maybe that young person is afraid their ideas will be shot down. Maybe they feel like their voice isn't powerful enough to make an impact. When we fully understand their hesitancy to speak out, we can help them strategize solutions.

11

Passion to Purpose

I WISH... I can help kids learn musis. I WISH this because music is a talent but people don't have the equiptment to learn.

I was not a born teacher. I did not set up my stuffed animals into little rows to teach them the alphabet. I was never the apple of any teacher's eye. In fact, I despised school.

There was no evidence in my childhood or adolescence that I would develop an interest in teaching. As a student, learning was merely transactional. If I completed the long list of worksheets and assignments and stayed out of trouble, I would pass the class. My mental image of a teacher was a polite, compliant, and sometimes stern lady. I was much too opinionated, loud, and angry to ever fit that mold.

When I was twenty-one years old, I started tutoring students in Washington, DC, as an AmeriCorps member. Working with kids became the highlight of my week. It lit me up in a way that nothing else had before. For me, it was more than just loving the interaction with students. Seeing the inequity in the American education system firsthand deeply angered me. I wanted to be a part of helping every child get the excellent education they deserve.

I enrolled in a teacher residency program. During my first weeks of class, two instructors in the program sat me down in a dimly lit room to tell me they did not think I was a good fit for their program. This devastated me, but it wasn't enough to deter me. I knew in my heart of hearts that teaching was my purpose. I just needed to develop the knowledge and skills to become an effective educator. I was not going to allow anyone's doubts stand in my way. It was never easy, but through hard work and the support of my lead teacher, I not only completed the program, but I excelled at it.

I carry that mindset with me into my own classroom. I constantly reflect on the day's events, and I take steps to make each lesson better. Whenever something goes wrong and I am disappointed in myself for making a mistake, a simple question has become my mantra, "Am I really mad I'm not perfect?" Internally, I know the answer. Following my passion is not easy. It takes a long time to perform at a high level. But no one is going to do the work for me. I have to do it myself.

I wanted my students to share this same mindset. We talk about not giving up, supporting others, and standing up for what you believe in. I don't want anyone's negative attitude to deter their dreams. I recount to my class that story of my instructors urging me to quit. My students were shocked. One boy, who was usually very quiet and reserved, replied in horror, "What? That's crazy! You have all the best books!"

I WISH FOR CHANGE

Nathaniel McGillivary,
seventeen-year-old student and
agricultural diesel mechanic

When I looked at that kid in the hallway, I saw myself. It wasn't just that we were both white kids growing up on the outskirts of Columbus, Ohio. It was the slumped shoulders, the fallen face, and the resigned stare. I asked him directly, "Do you even like school?"

He responded with a flat, "No. Not at all."

His response wasn't defiant; it was honest. It was a reality I knew all too well. A year ago, I would have said the exact same thing. At my old high school, I dreaded going to school each day. I was just another kid in the crowd. Nothing I did in class connected to the things I cared about, like cars and mechanics. I just didn't see the point of being there seven hours a day.

All that changed when I found the career center. When I first visited, I could not believe a place like this existed. Students spent half of the day in career labs and half of the day completing traditional high school classes.

On my first day in the diesel mechanic program, my teacher said, "This is not a classroom; it's a shop." We spent much of that first semester stripping engines down completely to the block, then building them back up until they ran again. We took courses on hydraulic and electrical systems as well as how to order parts and bill for our services.

(Continues)

(*I WISH FOR CHANGE*, *Nathaniel McGillivary Cont.*)

It wasn't just the shop that was different. One afternoon, I was completely lost in my traditional math class. My teacher saw the blank look on my face and walked over. He explained the problem to me as if it were a purchase order for auto parts, "Say you need to fix the car, and you have to figure out the parts you'll need. You can use this formula to find the exact quantity and cost." It's crazy how much math makes sense when it is connected to cars. I can even calculate the displacement of an engine: it's the bore squared times 0.7854 times the stroke length times the number of pistons.

If I would have never followed my love for mechanics to the career center, I would be stuck at my old high school just going through the motions. Now, everything has changed. I have found my life's work. My friends even joke that my personality changed. They say I used to look mad all the time. Now, I can't stop talking about my hopes and dreams for the future.

It kills me to think there are kids out there just like I used to be—stagnant, complacent, and hopeless. So I volunteer my time a couple days a month, going school to school and talking to kids about the career center. I want them to know there is a place out there where it's okay to be curious and enthusiastic.

When I was talking to that kid in the hallway, I just told him the truth. I said, "I've been where you are, but my life has completely changed. I can honestly tell you that I love school. I can't wait to go to class each day. I have a passion, and you can too."

Don't Find Your Passion, Develop It!

We are all born with an inherent passion. Our passion is there just waiting to be revealed. Once we correctly identify our passion, we discover an endless source of motivation and easily won success. Our specific passion is really the only thing worth pursuing in life.

We have all heard some version of those statements, but those beliefs could actually deter success. Researchers have found that "find your passion" can be bad advice because it undermines the development of people's interests. Professor Carol Dweck, who has famously described the growth mindset as the belief that one's abilities can improve through effort, is a part of a research team that has explored the connection between mindsets and perceptions of personal interests.

They found that people with a fixed mindset believed their passions to be constant and inherent, which actually has some bleak implications. First, this belief tends to narrow your focus and make you less open to learning about topics that don't align with your passions, which is problematic in an increasingly inter-disciplinary world. Say a young woman is passionate about web-site development. If she has a fixed mindset, she will be less willing to explore topics in the humanities, even though creating an effective website will require understanding of psychology, ar-tistic design, and even writing engaging copy.

Additionally, people who believe passions are predetermined and fixed are more likely to interpret setbacks as proof that a difficult pursuit could not possibly be a true passion. They falsely believe that true passions offer limitless motivation. It becomes easy for that young woman passionate in website development to discount her interest and quit pursuing it as soon as the going gets rough.

Is there a more helpful way to think about our passions? Rather than believing that interests are inherent, think of them as cultivated. It takes effort to develop a passion. It takes hard work, and that means you will experience challenges on your way to finding success. Dweck explained, "My undergraduates, at first, get all starry-eyed about the idea of finding their passion, but over time they get far more excited about developing their passion and seeing it through. They come to understand that that's how they and their futures will be shaped and how they will ultimately make their contributions."

> I wish I was a basket ball player and soccer player.

Try This . . .
TRIGGER THEIR INTEREST

How do people develop their individual interests? Why is one of my students obsessed with science fiction books and another student wants to read every poetry book on my shelf? Why does one teenager want to play hockey and another want to build robots?

Grounded in the theory that interests can indeed be developed, researchers Suzanne Hidi and K. Ann Renninger have attempted to answer this question through what they call the four phase model of interest development.

The first phase is to trigger their interest. We can help young people start the first phase by sharing new, exciting information. Once, a student was messing around when she was supposed to be reading. Instead of scolding her, I grabbed a book, flipped to the right page, and simply stated, "This lizard squirts blood out of its eyes." She grabbed the book and read it from cover to cover.

You can also trigger interest through personal relevance. I taught summer school one year, and the curriculum focused on insects. I bought plastic containers and assigned the kids homework: find some bugs and bring them to school. They were so excited to bring me tubs filled with ants, beetles, and centipedes. It set the stage for the rest of the learning because we were studying their own bugs.

The second phase is to maintain their interest. Once an interest is triggered, we can help young people further develop an interest by providing meaningful tasks. In science, I will teach basic electricity vocabulary, and then I will hand students a wire, a mini lightbulb, and a battery and tell them, "Light it up." Once they have figured out a simple circuit, I add in multiple wires and motors. Researchers also suggest that project-based learning, cooperative work, and individual tutoring can help maintain interest.

The third phase is identifying an individual interest that emerges. When a young person is at this stage, they have already built knowledge, and they value the opportunity to re-engage with the topic. They are actively, not forcefully,

(Continues)

(*TRY THIS, Trigger Their Interest Cont.*)

making a choice to explore this interest. Their curiosity deepens, and they become more persistent and resourceful. One student in my classroom was obsessed with dinosaurs. He didn't need my encouraging; he hunted down and read every dinosaur book I had. When we went to the museum on a field trip, he peppered a real paleontologist with a million questions.

The last phase is a robust and well-developed individual interest. This is the peak of interest development. It is a predisposition to engage with the same topic or content over a long period of time. Kids at this stage generate their own questions and seek their own answers. Young people can still benefit from adult support and positive feedback, but they are also self-motivated and will persevere, even in the face of frustration. This is the kid who teaches herself guitar in her room. This is the kid who authors entire comic books and builds inventions from scratch. We can support young people at this stage by continuing to provide challenges that lead to learning.

As caring adults, we play a role in helping young people progress through these phases. Without feedback, support, and opportunities to engage in an interest, a young person can remain stagnant in a lower phase or even regress. When we make space for a young person's curiosity, provide them with resources, and teach problem-solving strategies, they are more likely to chase their interests and develop passions.

I WISH... I can make it so dogs can live forever. I wish this because I love dogs.

Passion, Compassion, Action

Eighth-grader Aiden Horwitz has a love of all animals, and one dog in particular captured her heart. Royce was a muscular white American Cattle Dog with special needs. He had been in the animal shelter in Austin, Texas, for two years and still hadn't found a home. Aiden thought she could do something about it. When she started learning more about pet adoptions, she realized the reason why many pets end up in shelters is because they were not a good fit for their original owners.

Luckily, Aiden had the perfect opportunity to take action. Her school had a yearlong course called Passion Projects. Students spent one hour and fifteen minutes each week working on any project they chose. One student painted a mural, another created an escape room, and one girl started her own soap selling business. Aiden created DogDoOrDogDont.org.

Her website features a simple survey open to potential pet owners. She asks questions like these: How much barking can you tolerate? How long would the dog be home alone every day? And can you tolerate some damage to your furniture and clothes until your dog is trained?

A potential pet owner can view their results along with recommendations for adoptions, such as a dog in the hound group, the terrier group, older dogs, or even a result category titled "You might do better with cat." Potential pet owners can click a link that directs them to the website of a local animal shelter and the exact breed of dogs that would be a good fit for the respondent's lifestyle.

It was through Aiden's love of animals that she was able to recognize a pain point in the adoption process. Too many people were choosing the wrong dog. As Aiden explains on her website, "I wanted to come up with a way to help get dogs adopted or help people get the right dog for them and their family." Her passion for animals initiated her work, but it was the compassion for the dogs that did not have a loving home that drove her to action. Sydney followed the same passion, compassion, action model.

By the time Sydney Keys III was eleven years old, he had already developed a voracious appetite for books. His mom surprised him with a trip to Eye See Me, a bookstore that specializes in African American literature. He was delighted by what he saw—a whole store full of books with characters that looked like him. "I realized that there was a need for African American literacy and for boys to see themselves in books in a positive way. I wanted to share that with everyone else, too," Sydney explained in an interview. "Statistically, boys are behind in reading, and we wanted to combat against that stereotype where boys don't read as much as girls."

To respond to this problem, Sydney created Books N Bros, a book club for boys ages seven to thirteen years old. The bros read books from all genres, including *Hidden Figures*, *A Song for Harlem*, and *We Are the Ship: The Story of Negro League Baseball*. The boys meet up once a month, wearing their signature COOL

BROS READ T-shirts and discuss the book of the month. Adult mentors help facilitate discussions, and authors have even Skyped with the book club members. Sydney loved reading, but his love of reading alone did not create change. Change came when he recognized the challenges he faced were also faced by his peers. His empathy drove him to action.

Lily is another great example. At just seven years old, Lily Born noticed that her grandfather, who had Parkinson's disease, was having trouble drinking his coffee without spilling. She had the idea of adding three legs to his coffee cup so it wouldn't be able to tip over. That sent her to the kitchen where she added moldable plastic to an old plastic coffee cup. And the kangaroo cup was born.

After Lily made a successful prototype on a pottery wheel, her father not only encouraged her but helped put the cup into production. Lily and her dad traveled to China to find a manufacturer, launched several successful crowdfunding campaigns, and created a product that helps people around the world.

Lily hasn't just made a difference in the world; she has also changed herself. Once so shy that she wouldn't order for herself at a restaurant, Lily now speaks to rooms full of hundreds of investors and inventors, and has even presented her invention at the White House. Her story teaches us that when we help young people make a difference, they can not only transform the world, but they can also transform themselves.

We can help young people use their love of animals, literature, family, and so much more to fuel their desire to make a difference. All of these young people had a well-developed passion, and they also recognized a problem, such as a dog without a home, their peers not reading, or a cup that tipped over too often. Their compassion for others led them to take action and creatively solve problems. The next time a young person points out a cause of frustration, difficulty, or disappointment, we can ask: What do you want to do about it?

> I wish when I grow up I want to help my grandpa get some medicine to help his Kidny get back. I want to help his Kidney because I want him to practice baseball With me and swim' ride a bike and go fishing. I will have to be a scientist becase we have to test it out on some thing becase if we give it to him right away he will get him sick

MY POWER

Abby Williams,
11-year-old student

I guess you could say I love to be the center of attention. You can find me performing Shakespeare, making announcements during an assembly, hosting a class presentation on the solar system, or singing in the talent show. Most people at school know me for being on stage every opportunity I get. They also notice I use a wheelchair to get around. That's because I have Cerebral Palsy. But I don't let anything keep me from pursuing my passions. And my one true passion is fashion. I have always loved fashion, ever since I had the chance to model as a little girl. My favorite outfits are anything pink, purple, and sparkly because those are my favorite colors.

One day, my teacher and I came up with an idea. I could throw a schoolwide fashion show but with a twist. All the models would be kids with disabilities from my elementary school. I wanted to show the school that you can do anything, even model in a wheelchair.

My friends and I made announcements about the fashion show in all the classrooms and encouraged potential models to sign up. Then we hit the thrift store to pick out amazing clothes for the models to choose from. We decorated the auditorium with streamers and had the models select songs to strut their stuff to.

(Continues)

(MY POWER, Abby Williams Cont.)

After all that work, we were ready. When the fashion show started, I felt excited. In my opening speech, I said, "We all are different, and it's okay to be different. If we were all the same, life would be boring." Then it was time to roll out the red carpet. The music was pumping, and the audience of students and teachers were cheering like crazy.

There was a microphone at the end of the runway, and the models could introduce themselves and tell the crowd their disability if they wanted to. One kid said, "Hello my name is Denaysha, and I have Down syndrome." The auditorium erupted in applause." Another model said, "I don't learn math the way everyone else does." One of my friends used a voice app on her iPad to say her name. Even one of our teachers took to the catwalk saying, "I have ADHD, and I take medicine to help me concentrate." The crowd was so loud, I had to quiet them down a bunch of times.

One teacher told me later that a student in her class said the words "I have a learning disability" for the first time in his life. He said it into a microphone to his entire school while wearing an amazing suit and was greeted with a massive cheer.

The fashion show became an annual tradition. I wish more schools would do this because it would show kids with special needs they can do anything like write a book, model, or put on a show. Everyone deserves to follow their dreams, even down the runway.

I wish there was better technology to prevent illness,

Spark the Conversation

- What makes you excited to wake up in the morning?

- What are you curious about?

- How can you use your passions to make a difference?

When you talk to young people about what they care about, you will always learn something new. Once, I talked to a five-year-old who taught me how to count in Japanese and French.

Even if you may find the topic frivolous or simplistic, take the posture of a learner. Ask questions, be engaged, let the young person revel in their own knowledge—even if you already know a lot about the topic.

Start with specific, clear questions, and then move to more open-ended ones. If a kid loves video games, ask her what the rules of the game are and how points are earned. Then move on to questions like which strategies work best and who invented the game? You can take the conversation even deeper with questions like: Do the skills you practice in this game help you in other aspects of your life? How do you think the creator came up with the ideas for each level? When you ask these types of questions that help a young person explore their own curiosities and develop them into passions.

12

Assertiveness Sweet Spot

> I wish every one
> was president.

When my students walk down the hallway, I tell them, "Stand up straight. Shoulders back. Lift up your chin, not too much, but just enough so that everyone knows that kids in this line are very important. You have places to go and people to see."

All day long, I pour this idea into students. You are important. Your ideas matter. Speak up for yourself. Every day there are a hundred little opportunities for a kid to practice self-advocating—everything from keeping their spot in line, to asking to clarify directions, to standing up for a friend who is being picked on.

My goal is for kids to practice solving their own problems. When the sun is shining right in a boy's eyes, and he says, "Miss,

I can't see," my immediate response is to ask, "What can *you* do?" It sounds crazy, but it takes coaching to help a kid realize they can pull down the window shade.

Every year, I spend entire math lessons teaching how students can speak up when they don't understand something. Students need to know that the solution is not to sit there waiting for the teacher to notice that they are confused. Instead, each student needs to identify the specific part of the problem that is giving them trouble and ask for help. I also explicitly teach students what to do when their computer does not work, otherwise so many will sit there like a deer in headlights waiting for an adult to notice.

We talk about standing up in bigger ways, too. One of my favorite books to read aloud is *My Name is Maria Isabel* by Alma Flor Ada. It's a story of a girl who has to stand up to a teacher who is not saying her name correctly. Students take turns role-playing correcting someone who isn't saying their name correctly. I tell them explicitly, you might have to stand up for yourself with me this year. Just because I'm a teacher doesn't mean I can't make mistakes.

I've also worked with my school psychologist to teach a lesson about keeping our bodies safe and private. We talked about listening to your body and what to say when someone is making you feel uncomfortable. Then, the kids walked up to a piece of paper with a face drawn on it and practiced saying with conviction, "Don't touch me. I don't like it. I will tell an adult."

After years of working with children and seeing the same patterns of hesitancy I have realized that adults need to explicitly teach kids skills so they can stand up for themselves. We need to model and practice this. It all needs to happen in an environment where assertiveness is celebrated.

Molding Assertiveness

As a public school teacher, I learned pretty quickly to live by the saying, "Ask not, have not." No one was ever going to come around to my classroom just to check and make sure my students had everything they need. There has never been a magical closet of backpacks, school supplies, and classroom furniture up for grabs. If you need something, you have to ask. And I do. Often. I have asked for everything from theater tickets to toothpaste for my students. In fact, if you took out everything from my classroom that I had to ask for, you would be left with one rug, ten tables, and a Promethean board. Everything else, and I mean everything, had to be asked for.

To get what I need for my students, I have to be bold and assertive but not too bold and assertive. When you are asking for something, whether it is school supplies, a raise, or a new policy, you can't be timid, but you also can't be brash.

Finding that balance can be difficult, and just like everything else in life it takes practice. The good news is, researchers agree that assertiveness is a learned skill and a very valuable one. In fact, "People who have mastered the skill of assertiveness are able to greatly reduce the level of interpersonal conflict in their lives, thereby reducing a major source of stress."

For most people, and I very much include myself, it can be difficult to self-assess your own level of assertiveness. Researchers at Columbia University found there is a consistent mismatch between personal perception of your assertiveness and the perception of others. Studies found that most people who thought they were being appropriately or under assertive were actually seen as overly assertive by others. And the reverse is also true. If adults are bad at monitoring their own level of assertiveness, how can we teach young people to stand up for themselves, advocate for their needs, and do so in ways that get results?

First, it's helpful to teach young people exactly what assertiveness is. Assertiveness is often confused with being demanding, aggressive, or dogmatic. However, being truly assertive is not negative at all. In research, assertiveness is typically defined as "the legitimate and honest expression of one's personal rights, feelings, beliefs, and interest without violating or denying the rights of others." The central question we should teach young people to ask is, can you express your thoughts and opinions, while also respecting the opinions of others?

Another way we can help is by giving loving feedback. I remember at the end of a graduate class, a professor pulled me aside and said, "You have a lot of great ideas to contribute, but you trail off at the end of every thought." She was right. I and many other women in my classes had learned the social script that told us to qualify every thought with phrases such as, "That's just my opinion," "You know what I mean?" "Sorry, I could be wrong," or the ubiquitous, "Um . . . yeah." It became so ingrained that I was not even aware of it. I remember my professor said, "You need to be like an airplane pilot, confident and clear. Imagine if the pilot said, 'Buckle your seat belts . . . um . . . that's, like, just what I think." Her feedback was so effective for me. It was clear and concise but also communicated that she cared about me and wanted my communication skills to improve.

Now, I try to provide that same loving feedback to my students. Like most things in my classroom, it starts with a relationship. For young people, feedback without a relationship is usually perceived as criticism. If I want my feedback to be received, kids have to know I care about them.

Every year, there are always two or three students who are clearly terrified to give the wrong answer in class. Their self-doubt is palpable. To help them gain confidence, I use a simple phrase, "You are right; say it like you are right." This encourages the student and alleviates anxiety but also gives them a clear next step.

For those kids who are coming on too strong, I follow the same strategy of validating them as a person yet coaching their delivery. I'll say, "Pause. You are not a rude person. Notice how you sound. Try not to be rude on accident." I remember one day a kid was absent-mindedly blocking the bookshelf, and another kid shouted, "Move! Get out of my way!" My response was serious but clear. I said, "That is exactly how you should talk if there is a fire, but we are not in a fire. We are in a classroom. So, how can you say that in a way that works in a classroom?" The idea is not to stamp out assertiveness, but to mold it so kids can advocate for their needs more effectively.

Finally, research shows assertiveness is just as much about what we say to ourselves as what we say to others. If a young person is thinking, "My idea will never work" or "Who would listen to me anyway?" that negative self-talk will impact their ability to communicate their ideas effectively. I talk to kids about listening to their internal voice. I teach kids to ask the simple question: Is that voice lying or telling the truth? Once young people can identify negative thoughts, we teach them to replace them with more positive thoughts like, "My idea could be good, I should share it" and "I know a lot about this, so I should speak up."

Through defining assertiveness, delivering loving feedback, and examining self-talk, we can help young people mold their assertiveness and find the sweet spot. The spot where they can confidently advocate for their needs, empathetically listen to the needs of others, and make a difference in the world.

MY POWER

Andrea Valverde Hernandez,
sixteen-year-old student

I'm sure the rest of the students in my tenth-grade literature class saw that day as no different than the day before
it, but for me it was monumental. I just could not stay silent
anymore. There was something inside that was saying,
"Speak up. Say what you think." For once, I did.

The whole class was reading "Gilgamesh"—the epic
poem from ancient Mesopotamia—and discussing the
namesake character. I was one of only a handful of girls in
that class. The boys, most of whom were white and middle
class, were dominating the conversation. They all thought
that, after failing yet another trial, Gilgamesh felt simply
disappointed.

I saw something in Gilgamesh they did not see. I saw
that he was not experiencing disappointment; he was having a crisis of confidence. He was consumed by self-doubt.
Would he be able to overcome the seemingly insurmount-
able challenges that lay ahead of him? Or were his fate and
his failure already decided?

I recognized this inner turmoil in Gilgamesh because I
saw it in myself. Teachers are always warning teenagers
about the "real world." The truth is, I have already experienced more real world than most of my teachers. I knew
the anxious hum of wondering where I would sleep some
nights. I knew the stifled pain of being judged by the

Mexican accent in my voice. I knew the ever-present fear of my family being separated. The real world is not a distant eventuality. It was a place I navigated every day. Like Gilgamesh, I wondered if my efforts would be enough to see me through life's never-ending trials.

At that point in my life, I felt like I was protecting myself in a bubble of my own making. If I talked in class, I was barely able to be heard. When I spoke at all, it was to quickly agree with someone else's idea and hope the discussion would move on as soon as possible. Somehow that day, in that lesson about a strong, yet hesitant hero, I found my voice. I made a bold move to share my own ideas with the class. I found the courage to disagree, to share my perspective, and to speak my truth.

It seems so small, but that little expression planted a seed of conviction in me. It was nourished by my teacher who followed up with me after class to tell me he was grateful I shared my perspective with the class. From that grew the realization that I had something to say and others needed to hear it. I wanted to express myself, to share my lived experience, and to connect to others who could relate. That's when I got the idea to start Latino Club. I hoped to create a space where students could feel empowered in their identity and share their culture.

In Latino Club, we had two main goals. First, we wanted to share our experience with our classmates and teach them about the culture we cherished. We did this by celebrating Latin American holidays and inviting others to join in. When Puerto Rico was devastated both by Hurricane

(Continues)

(MY POWER, Andrea Valverde Hernandez Cont.)

Maria and by the insufficient response of the United States government, we taught our classmates about it through a schoolwide presentation and hosted a fundraiser.

Our second goal was to have a native Spanish speaker teaching our Spanish language classes. Not only did we want our teacher with a high level of language competency, we also wanted someone who understood the experience of being bilingual, someone who could relate to our lives as Spanish speakers from the inside. Being a part of a group gave me the confidence to share my concerns with the director of the school. I wasn't just standing up for myself, I was standing up for my community. After a year of advocating, the school's next hire for the position was indeed a native Spanish speaker.

Those victories, small at first, built on each other. Now I feel I can speak my mind, my ideas are worth sharing, and my work can make a difference.

I wish that the whole world can sign like deaf people so it's easy to communicate with hearing people also my family is deaf and i see them strugling with hearing people and i try to help also in the future I want to own a deaf company.

Taking a Stand

When kids stand up for themselves, they often stand up for others in the process. I tell kids if something is bothering you, it's probably bothering other people, too. Solving your own problems often means you are making a difference for others. This is exactly what happened with Grace Warnock from Scotland.

"In my job, lots of people come to me with problems," said Iain Gray, member of the Scottish Parliament. "Far fewer come with problems and a solution they're suggesting. Fewer still come with a problem and a solution, and the determination to make that solution actually happen. An exception to that rule though is Grace Warnock."

Grace Warnock looks like any average ten-year-old, but she is living with Crohn's disease, a chronic inflammatory bowel condition. It causes her to makes frequent trips to the restroom. Too often, when Grace uses the disability accessible toilet, she is met with criticism from onlookers because she does not fit their stereotypes of what a person who is disabled looks like.

Instead of simply ignoring these misplaced judgments, Grace decided to stand up for herself. She started a campaign with the goal of raising awareness about invisible disabilities. She started this with an idea for a new, improved bathroom sign. Grace's accessible toilet sign features the standard icon of a person in a wheelchair that we are all familiar with, but the icons of a man and a woman with a red heart in the middle of their chests are also featured. Underneath are the words, "Not all conditions are visible. Please be patient with everyone using these facilities."

Grace has convinced airports, offices, shopping malls, and even the Scottish Parliament to hang her sign on their accessible toilets. She succeeded in making the daily lives of people with

disabilities a little easier and making her community more welcoming. She also started a wider conversation about the precon-
ceived notions and biases that exist about disabilities. Through
standing up for herself, she was able to create change in a larger
way. The same is true of Marley Dias.

One day over pancakes, Marley's mom asked her what she
would change if she could change anything in the world. What
she really wanted, as Marley recounts in her book, *Marley Dias
Gets It Done (And So Can You!)* was, "A world where modern black
girls were the main characters—not invisible, not just the side-
kick. A world where black girls were free to be complicated, honest, human; to have adventures and emotions unique just to them.
A world where black girls' stories mattered."

Marley's world was very different than the one she dreamed up.
At school she had been assigned to read *Old Yeller, Where the Red
Fern Grows,* and *Shiloh*—an endless stream of books about white
boys and their dogs, she noted. For Marley, "Frustration is fuel that
can lead to the development of an innovative and useful idea."

At just twelve years old, Marley started the social media campaign #1000BlackGirlBooks with the goal of collecting and dis-
tributing one thousand books featuring black female characters.
She far surpassed her goal, created an online database of books,
and is even developing an app and creating a global book club.

So many children experience the same challenges as Marley,
and through her leadership and assertiveness, schools, educators,
and communities are examining diverse representation in children's literature. Marley is an example for how young people can
take local problems and find global solutions. That's what happened for David and Travis.

David Shepherd and Travis Price were just two high school
students in a small town in Nova Scotia, Canada, when they saw

a younger classmate being teased for wearing a pink polo shirt. The boys decided to take a stand. They encouraged their friends to wear pink and bought fifty pink tank tops at the local discount shop. On the planned day, the school halls were lined with kids wearing pink and standing up against bullying. When the younger student walked in and saw a sea of pink, "It looked like a huge weight was lifted off his shoulders," Travis recalled. "I learned that two people can come up with an idea, run with it, and it can do wonders."

Their idea did indeed do wonders. From that day back in 2007 to now, Pink Shirt Day has become a global campaign. Not only does it inspire young people to show kindness and empathy toward others, but the campaign has also raised more than $1.8 million Canadian. They put the funds toward anti-bullying programming and youth support services through organizations like the YMCA, the Boys & Girls Club, and suicide prevention hotlines.

Grace, Marley, David, and Travis used their personal experiences to launch campaigns that helped others far beyond their community. One young person's insight and courage can be someone else's hope.

MY WISH FOR THE WORLD

Matthew Morris, teacher and author

Reflection. It has changed the trajectory of my life. It shaped me as an educator. It is a tool I give my students.

I followed my dreams down a football field all the way from the east end of Toronto to a college scholarship. When I blew out my shoulder, that journey was over. Internal questions began to percolate. If football was not an option, if money was not an object, and if I could do anything, what would I do with my life? An answer came from somewhere within me. I wanted to make a positive impact on the young people in my community. That simple reflection sent me on a new path—to study to become a teacher.

While earning my credentials to teach, much of my learning was in examining myself. When I looked back on my own schooling, I could see how carefully I curated an image of myself as a defiant student. I showed up late to class. I refused to follow rules that limited my expression, and wore a hat and headphones always.

For the first time I was able to see those choices were not motivated by disrespect, but rather were an attempt to assert my own identity. I sought validation from teachers. I craved recognition from my peers. The hip hop culture I loved exuded from me, but it was always met with disapproval at school. As an adult, I could now recognize the undercurrent of tension between the school system's expectations and my own desire to assert my identity as a young, black male.

As a teenager, I felt so devalued by a teacher that I slipped a sentence into the middle of an essay. It read, "I know you don't read what I write. Just give me the same bad grade you always do." When my teacher handed back my essay, I didn't get the reaction I was hoping for. I didn't get any reaction at all. At the top of my paper, in red pen it simply said, "60%." I knew I never wanted my students to feel the way I felt that day.

The day finally came when I stood in front of my very own classroom, in the same middle school I once attended. Having a student call me "Mr. Morris" for the first time was one of the most rewarding and humbling moments of my life. I wanted to give each student the same encouragement, support, and validation that I had once sought.

I established Family Time Friday. It is a thirty-minute chunk of time when my class comes together to discuss our lives, interests, and experience. Topics vary, but inevitably the dialogue circles back to the concept equity. We have talked about current events, political decisions, and stereotypes in advertising.

I decided to leverage this group reflection in my lessons. I assigned the class to write essays on how the students experience equity or the lack thereof. I was blown away by the level of care and effort the class put in. One student penned an explanation of why, as a young Muslim, she had chosen not to wear a hijab. Another girl wrestled

(Continues)

(MY WISH FOR THE WORLD, Matthew Morris Cont.)

with the idea of how domestic violence has impacted her life. One boy wrote about the lack of diverse representation in Hollywood films. Each student displayed a critical consciousness that was born from our class discussions.

After those essays, I noticed a change in how my students interacted with me. One day in science class, students were engineering a model bridge. A group of girls asked to swap out the egg carton they were given because it still had dried-on pieces of shell inside. Without thinking, I remarked, "Girls are always so particular." That group of young women called me out in front of the whole class. Our lessons stopped as, one by one, the girls informed me of the gender bias in my comment.

I was not proud of my comment, but I was proud of their reaction. They were right. They had the moral authority and confidence to challenge me when I was wrong.

When young people can speak out in our classrooms, they build the skills to do so later in life. Those young women will not tolerate bias in the workplace. They will be assertive and speak out when they see discrimination in the community. If we want young people to stand up for themselves, we must empower them to reflect on their own life experiences and deliberately create space for their concerns to be heard.

I wish we would acknowledge the brilliance in all cultures, seek to learn from each other, and strive to validate our youth in all possible ways.

There are situations in every young person's life that requires them to stand up for themselves. When young people have the skills to be assertive, active members of their community they can have a far-reaching impact.

It is important to remember, if we want a generation of young people who challenge injustice and speak truth to power, those young people need to be heard. This means we need to listen and become safe, responsive sounding boards for the concerns and innovations. We, caring adults, should amplify their voices and champion their causes.

Spark the Conversation

- Have you ever wanted to tell me something but felt like you couldn't?

- Do you think you are over assertive, under assertive, or just assertive enough?

- What makes it tricky for people to stand up for themselves?

- How does it feel when you do express your feelings and ideas?

One worry I have as a teacher is that a student in my classroom has something they need to tell me but are hesitant for some reason. I explicitly state several times during each school year that I am someone they can trust. I will listen to them without judgment, and I will be a partner in problem solving. So many adults have this same mindset, and young people need to hear this clearly and consistently. If we neglect to, there may be a young person in our lives who is holding a painful or difficult secret but is afraid to speak up.

Once we establish an element of trust and openness in our relationships with young people, we can help them identify times when they can stand up for themselves. We can help teach them the skills they need to do just that and provide opportunities to practice. Be honest with young people that speaking up for themselves and their communities is often just a first step. They will have to be assertive and confident enough to raise concerns but will also need to take action if they want to see changes.

Conclusion

> I wish there was and Is WORLD PEACE, No violence, no fights just Peace, no stealing, Just PEACE.

On a hot Friday afternoon, the six-foot-tall sunflowers drooped with a head full of seeds. The grapevine my mom planted six years earlier had finally bore fruit, and the weeds were starting to creep into the vegetable beds of our school garden. I gathered all my students in a lopsided circle. In the middle was a green pop-up enclosure with a zipper on the top. It was time.

The kids had spent weeks watching as little black caterpillars munched on their food. They shared squeals of excitement when they returned to the classroom after lunch to find that all of the once wiggly caterpillars had formed tight-grey chrysalises. A few days later I stopped a math lesson mid-sentence to watch a wrinkled butterfly emerge and stretch out its wings.

Now was the time to let the butterflies fly free. Circled up with my class, I thought to myself, this is a moment my students will remember. I have to make it special, make some sort of ceremony out of it. I told the kids, "Sometimes when people release butterflies, they say something important like their hopes or dreams. Do you want to try?"

A couple of kids raised their hands. "I hope people will treat each other nicely," said one little boy. Another kid shouted out, "I hope people will respect nature and stop pollution." We went around the circle and more hopes came spilling out. "I hope they stop having wars," said a boy. "I hope people stop drinking alcohol." "I hope no one goes to jail." "I hope no one hurts any more animals." "I hope everyone has a friend and no one is lonely."

When the last kids shouted out their hopes. I stepped forward and unzipped the butterfly enclosure. "We should say something special. What should it be?" I asked the class. A girl cried out, "Release hope to the world!" The whole class shouted it, the butterflies flew up and away, and a trail of children chased them across the field.

As the kids chased the butterflies, their comments flew around in my head. It was so simple for them to voice their hopes. They were only eight years old yet already had experienced enough to know the world is an imperfect place. Their hopes

> I wish people would take care of each
> each other and our sorronding. Make the
> world beataful.

ticked off a list of societal ills and personal challenges. Still, their reservoirs of optimism made it so simple to wish for a better world.

My students are so much like the little caterpillars, experiencing the world as they grow stronger each day. Soon, they will fly free into an uncertain world. I have hopes for them myself. I hope they treat others fairly and expect the same in return. I hope they make decisions based on their values and find a community that encourages them. And I hope they pursue their passions and stand up for what they believe in.

I also have some hopes for us adults. I hope we share our wisdom and knowledge generously. That we use our words not just to assert our authority, but also to share it. That we help young people embrace their interests and explore their curiosities. That we empathize with the challenges young people face and nurture their tendencies toward compassion.

Many caring adults are already doing this work. To them, I say thank you for being a supportive, encouraging force in a young person's life. There are many of us who want to continue what you have started.

We have the tools to do this, many of which are included in this book. But many of our tools to support the young people in our lives are intuitive. We can ask probing questions, validate frustration, and offer words of encouragement. When a young person has an idea to make a difference, we can simply ask: Why not you? Why not now?

By doing so, children won't have to wish for change. They will make it.

I wish that people were all Safe. I hope that one day everyone can live in peace, and feel safe in there own homes. One day I want to see everyone smiling not worrying. I hope one day my wish will come true.

Join the
#IWishForChange Community

We can provide young people with a sense of community—a place where they are free to share ideas and engage with others who wish for change. As adults, we can also benefit from a supportive community of our own. People of any age can use the power of community to share strategies and insights that help us create change in our communities, whether that change is individual or will affect the whole world.

I urge every reader of this book to reach out to the young people in their lives, to find out their passions and their hopes for the future. As you are helping those young folks chase down their dreams, share your own journey with others. Let us know how you have helped young people advocate for their needs, advance their ideas for solutions and navigate complex systems of power in order to make a real difference.

Join our community today by visiting **www.iwishforchange book.com** and using **#IWishForChange** hashtag on social media. You can reach out to me directly **@kylemschwartz** on Twitter and Instagram. Together we can turn young people's wishing into realities. We can talk, share, and dream of a better world. Together we can help every young person unleash their power to make a difference.

Acknowledgments

So many people deserve acknowledgment for helping to make this book a reality. Thank you to my editor, Dan Ambrosio, for believing in the power of young people and envisioning a book with the same message. I would also like to thank my agent Lynn Johnston, who has helped me every step of the way. To everyone at Da Capo Lifelong, thank you for all the work it took to get this book to readers. I would also like to extend my gratitude to my collaborator and friend, Meghan Stevenson. Your ability to help others share their stories has made the world a better place.

To the many people and organizations that helped me on my path to becoming a teacher, thank you. I would also like to thank Equity Network United for Denver for helping me make a difference in my own community.

As proud public school teacher, I would like to thank all the people who make Doull Elementary the best school I've ever been to, especially our compassionate principal, Jodie Carrigan, who believed in me before I was even a teacher and has helped our school become a beacon of light. Thank you also to all my fellow teachers and staff at Doull, all of whom work every single day in service of our students. To the families who have supported my classroom and given me the privilege of teaching their children, thank you.

I would like to thank all the young people who have lent their stories to this book—some I have known for many years, while others I've just met and had the opportunity to learn from. All of you have given myself and the readers of this book so much to consider and countless reasons to hope for a better future. To the caring educators, researchers, advocates, and organizers who not only shared their wisdom and insight but have also been a champion for young people in your community—thank you for holding others up.

I owe a thank you to the friends and family members who have offered me unwavering support and encouragement: J. J. Schuber, Benafsha Shroff, Kathy Brougham, Rachel Bernard, Angela Cobian, Lauren Fine, Molly Couture, Val Wintler, and Gilbert Blythe. Thank you for listening, asking questions, and providing insight. Thank you also to Beth Tidwell and Shift Workspaces for providing a wonderful place to write.

Finally, I would like to thank my family. To my grandmother Darlene Schwartz who always makes sure I know I am cared about. To all the Schwartzes and Galbraiths out there, having a family that lives with integrity and generosity has made such an impression on my life.

I would like to thank Katelyn who is a dedicated educator and wonderful sister. Finally, all my gratitude goes to my parents. I don't deserve the best parents in the world, but I got them, anyway. My father, who is known to all the students at our school as Coach Ken, and my mother, Cathy, who taught me by example to put others first. I love you all very, very much.

Notes

Introduction

2 **the napkin industry**: Richie Norton, "The 14 Most Destructive Millennial Myths Debunked by Data," January 9, 2017, *The Mission Podcasts*. Retrieved from https://medium.com /the-mission/the-14-most-destructive-millennial-myths -debunked-by-data-aa00838eecd6.

Chapter 1

10 **toward change**: Author interview with Jennifer Bacon, July 17, 2018.

10 **positively or negatively**: Cameron Anderson, Oliver P. John, and Dacher Keltner, "The Personal Sense of Power," *Journal of Personality*, April 2012. Retrieved from www.haas.berkeley.edu /faculty/papers/anderson/jopy734.pdf.

11 **The Daily Beast**: Tanya Basu, "This Kid Single-Handledly Ignited the Plastic Straw Ban Movement," *Daily Beast*, July 24, 2018. Retrieved from www.thedailybeast.com/this-kid-single-handedly -launched-the-plastic-straw-ban-movement.

11 **use plastic straws**: Author interview with Milo Cress, November 25, 2018.

11 **drink automatically**: "Be Straw Free: Take Action With Each One Reach One Approach," 2016. Retrieved from www.ecocycle.org /bestrawfree/one.

14 **intelligence or "normalcy"**: Lisa D. Delpit, "The Silenced Dia- logue: Power and Pedagogy in Education Other People's Children," *Harvard Educational Review*, August 1988. Retrieved from http://lmcreadinglist.pbworks.com/f/Delpit+(1988).pdf.

14   **interests of students:** Seth Kreisberg, *Transforming Power* (New York: SUNY Press, 1992).

15   *Get Up or Give Up*: Michael Bonner, *Get Up or Give Up: How I Almost Gave Up on Teaching* (Brentwood, TN: Post Hill Press, 2017).

16   **as human beings:** Author interview with Michael Bonner,

17   **its existence:** Delpit, "The Silenced Dialogue."

Chapter 2

20   **irresponsibility and irrational thinking:** Adora Svitak, "What Adults Can Learn From Kids," TED Talks, February 2010. Retrieved www.ted.com/talks/adora_svitak/transcript.

21   **purpose in life:** Andrew Martin, "Coping with Change: Teaching Adaptability Will Help Kids Grow," *The Conversation*, November 10, 2013. Retrieved from https://theconversation.com/coping -with-change-teaching-adaptability-will-help-kids-grow-19726.

27   **in an interview:** Steve Hartman. "4-Year-Old Superhero Using His Power to Feed the Homeless," CBS News, May 4, 2018. Retrieved from www.cbsnews.com/news/austin-perine-alabama-4-year-old -superhero-using-his-power-to-feed-the-homeless.

29   **My Wish for the World:** Contributed by Angela Cobián

31   **contamination in water:** Katie Kindelan, "11-Year-Old Girl Inspired by Flint Water Crisis Creates Cheap Kit to Test Lead," ABC News, October 18, 2017. Retrieved from https://abcnews. go.com/Lifestyle/11-year-girl-inspired-flint-water-crisis-creates /story?id=50559884.

32   **stay silent anymore:** Author interview with Sunrose Guerrero, September 17, 2018.

33   **says Dr. Simmons:** Author interview with Dr. Dena Simmons, September 11, 2018.

34   **someone is powerful:** Vivian Gussin Paley, *The Kindness of Children* (Cambridge, MA: Harvard University Press, 2000, revised ed.).

Chapter 3

37   **on the playground**: Christian's Buddy Bench. Retrieved from http://buddybench.org.

38   **eating lunch alone**: Sit With Us. Retrieved from http://www.sitwithus.io/#!/About.

38   **begin with lunch**: Ibid.

39   **the next table over**: Natalie Hampton, "All It Takes Is One," TEDxTeen. Retrieved from www.tedxteen.com/talks/all-it-takes-is-one-natalie-hampton.

39   **food, water, and safety**: A. H. Maslow, "A Theory of Human Motivation," *Psychological Review*, 1943.

39   **adverse conditions**: Roy F. Baumeister and Mark R. Leary, "The Need to Belong: A Desire for Interpersonal Attachments as a Fundamental Human Motivation," *Psychological Bulletin*, 1995.

41   **loved and needed**: Contributed by Ally Vincent, July 20, 2018.

42   **is mutual**: Baumeister and Leary, "The Need to Belong."

44   **for the disruption**: Christopher Emdin, *For White Folks Who Teach in the Hood . . . and the Rest of Y'all Too* (Boston: Beacon Press, 2016).

47   **can embrace others**: Contributed by Joe Dombrowski, July 30, 2018.

48   **my teaching career**: Author interview with Lynn Malie, October 28, 2018.

48   **little consequence**: Baumeister and Leary, "The Need to Belong."

49   **such as schoolwork**: Author interview with Mark R. Leary, July 11, 2018.

49   **better in school**: Carissa Romero, "What We Know About Belonging From Scientific Research," *Mindset Scholars Network*, July 2015. Retrieved from http://mindsetscholarsnetwork.org/wp-content/uploads/2015/09/What-We-Know-About-Belonging.pdf.

50　**originated in 1996**: Irene S. Levine, "BFF Makes the Oxford English Dictionary," *Huffington Post*, September 17, 2010. Retrieved from www.huffingtonpost.com/irene-s-levine/bff-makes-the-oxford-engl_b_721814.html.

51　**who you are**: Brene Brown, *Braving the Wilderness* (New York: Random House, 2017).

Chapter 4

54　**more than a peer**: Katherine McAuliffe, Peter R. Blake, and Felix Warneken, "Do Kids Have a Fundamental Sense of Fairness?" *Scientific American*, August 23, 2017. Retrieved from https://blogs.scientificamerican.com/observations/do-kids-have-a-fundamental-sense-of-fairness.

58　**all children**: Contributed by Elizabeth Kleinrock, July 10, 2018.

61　**evasion and deception**: "Punishment vs. Logical Consequences," Responsive Classroom Newsletter, August 1998. Retrieved from www.responsiveclassroom.org/punishment-vs-logical-consequences.

62　**supportive atmosphere**: Ibid.

63　**makes others feel**: "Cameron's Anti-Bully Campaign." Retrieved from http://antibullycampaign.org/club.html.

63　**prevent bullying**: Julie Farren, "Seeing the Error of His Ways, Second-Grader Starts Anti-Bullying Club," *Record Gazette*, June 6, 2014. Retrieved from www.recordgazette.net/news/schools/article_eb733e02-ecd4-11e3-a138-001a4bcf887a.html.

Chapter 5

68　**students' revisions**: Romero, "What We Know About Belonging From Scientific Research."

69　**with belief**: Maureen Healy, "Confidence in Children," *Psychology Today*, March 11, 2009. Retrieved from www.psychologytoday.com/us/blog/creative-development/200903/confidence-in-children.

70   **across a lifespan**: E. H. Erikson, *Identity, Youth, and Crisis* (New York: Norton, 1968).

71   **Erikson's Psychosocial Stages Abbreviated**: [Adapted from] Erikson, *Identity, Youth, and Crisis.*

75   **of encouragement**: Author interview with Joseph Matthews, October 1, 2018.

75   **young lady**: Scott Berson, "Third Grader Was Born With No Hands—and Just Won an Award for Her Cursive Writing," *Miami Herald*, May 10, 2018. Retrieved from www.miamiherald.com /news/nation-world/national/article210869984.html.

77   **she explained**: Brian Hill, "Chesapeake Child Born Without Hands Uses Penmanship to Overcome Challenges," WTKR, May 9, 2018. Retrieved from https://wtkr.com/2018/05/09 /chesapeake-child-born-without-hands-using-penmanship -to-overcome-challenges.

Chapter 6

79   **successes and failures**: Dr. Raymond P. Perry, research focus, Psychology Department, University of Manitoba. Retrieved from http://home.cc.umanitoba.ca/~maach/perryresearch.html.

80   **shorter lifespans**: Ibid.

80   **learning conditions**: Tara L. Haynes, Raymond P. Perry, Robert H. Stupnisky, and Lia M. Daniels, "A Review of Attributional Retraining Treatments: Fostering Engagement and Persistence in Vulnerable College Students," *Higher Education: Handbook of Theory and Research* (New York: Springer, 2009).

81   **individual role**: Wade Gilbert, "Finding and Building Coachable Athletes," *Human Kinetics*, April 21, 2015. Retrieved from www.humankinetics.com/all-coaching-and-officiating -articles/all-coaching-and-officiating-articles/ finding-and-building-coachable-athletes.

82   **other people**: Anderson, John, and Keltner, "The Personal Sense of Power."

83   **other relationships**: Author interview with Cameron Anderson, June 10, 2018.

84   **powerless parents**: Daphne Blunt Bugental and Jeffrey Clayton Lewis, "The Paradoxical Misuse of Power by Those Who See Themselves as Powerless: How Does It Happen?" *Journal of Social Issues,* 1999.

84   **misunderstanding and conflict**: Ibid.

85   **of a C+**: Haynes, Perry, Stupnisky, and Daniels. "A Review of Attributional Retraining Treatments."

86   **"can-do" attitude**: Ibid.

89   **ignore it**: Adam D. Galinsky, Deborah H. Gruenfeld, and Joe C. Magee, "From Power to Action," *Journal of Personality and Social Psychology,* 2003. Retrieved from https://pdfs.semanticscholar. org/5883/beaa6f64aeb216b97575f35ca52a743e1284.pdf.

Chapter 7

99   **the *Washington Post***: Allison Klein, "This City Just Passed an Anti-Smoking Law. It's the Brainchild of a Girl Scout Troup," *Washington Post,* March 9, 2018. Retrieved from www .washingtonpost.com/news/inspired-life/wp/2018/03/09 /this-city-just-passed-an-antismoking-law-it-was-written -by-a-girl-scout-troop/?utm_term=.881796d03bd7

99   **worth a try**: Author interview with Makenna Batcho, August 26, 2018.

100 **said Cassandra**: Cassandra Lin, "TGIF! Turn Grease Into Fuel. My Name My Story," 2015. Retrieved from http://myname mystory.org/cassandra-lin.html.

101 **stop there**: Project TGIF. Retrieved from www.projecttgif.com.

101 **the world!**: Lin. "TGIF! Turn Grease Into Fuel."

102 **called FWFWFLFH**: Dave Beckwith, with Christina Lopez, "Community Organizing: People Power from the Grassroots. Center for Community Change." Retrieved from https://comm-org.wisc.edu/papers97/beckwith.htm.

104   **courage to act**: Marshall Ganz, "What is Public Narrative: Self, Us, & Now," (working paper). Retrieved from https://dash.harvard .edu/bitstream/handle/1/30760283/Public-Narrative-Worksheet -Fall-2013-.pdf?sequence=1.

109   **work continues**: Contributed by Salem Atsbha Hailu, July 13, 2018.

Chapter 8

115   **change the world**: Contributed by Naomi O'Brien, July 24, 2018.

118   **any state**: "Colorado Experience: KKK," PBS, aired January 19, 2017. Retrieved from www.pbs.org/video/colorado-experience-kkk.

118   **pistol-whipped**: Julie Turkewitz, "Family History Haunts G.O.P. Candidate for Governor in Colorado," *New York Times*, July 24, 2018. Retrieved from www.nytimes.com/2018/07/24/us/colorado -governor-stapleton.html.

119   **in a PBS documentary**: "Colorado Experience: KKK."

119   **namesake**: Author interview with P. J. Shields, August 1, 2018.

120   **to embody**: Meredith Turk, "A Stapleton Middle School Tackles the KKK Connection in Their Name," Colorado Public Radio, May 31, 2018. Retrieved from www.cpr.org/news/story/a-stapleton- middle-school-tackles-the-kkk-connection -in-their-name.

120   **this issue**: Author interview with P. J. Shields.

Chapter 9

127   **skills and strategies**: Paula Denton, *Learning Through Academic Choice* (Turners Falls, MA: Center for Responsive Schools, 2005).

131   **more fun**: "Are You Offering Your Children Too Many Choices?" KelloggInsight, September 5, 2017. Retrieved from https://insight. kellogg.northwestern.edu/article/choice-set-size-and-children.

132   **or the author**: Irene C. Foutnas and Gay Su Pinnell, "Guided Reading: The Romance and the Reality," *The Reading Teacher*

(New York: Heinemann, 2012). Retrieved from www.heinemann.
com/fountasandpinnell/supportingmaterials/fountaspinnell
_revdreadingteacherarticle12_2012.pdf.

134   **competence, and relatedness**: Idit Katz and Avi Assor, "When
Choice Motivates and When It Doesn't," *Educational Psychology
Review*, 2006.

Chapter 10

138   **Harvard Graduate School of Education**: Leah Shafer, "Giving
Students A Voice," Usable Knowledge, August 18, 2016. Retrieved
from www.gse.harvard.edu/news/uk/16/08/giving-students-voice.

139   **perspectives bring**: Ibid.

143   **voice count**: Contributed by Ahmed Eltayeb, August 6, 2018.

145   **democracy by lecture**: Alfie Kohn, "Choices for Children:
Why and How to Let Students Decide," 1993. Retrieved from
www.alfiekohn.org/article/choices-children.

145   **participatory democracy**: Nelson Beaudoin, *Elevating Student
Voice: How to Enhance Student Participation, Citizenship, and
Leadership* (New York: Eye on Education, 2005; Routledge, 2013).

146   **the Spectrum of Public Participation**: Adapted from iap2 public
participation spectrum, International Association for Public Public
Participation Australasia. Retrieved from www2.fgcu.edu/Provost
/files/IAP_Public_Participation_Spectrum.pdf.

147   **explained to me**: Author interview with Candi DiBeca,
August 28, 208.

153   **embrace all voices**: Contributed by Desmond Williams,
July 27, 2018.

Chapter 11

158   **you can too**: Contributed by Nathaniel McGillivary, August 20,
2018.

159   **people's interests**: Paul A. O'Keefe, Carol S. Dweck, and Gregory
M. Walton, "Implicit Theories of Interest: Finding Your Passion or
Developing It?" *Psychological Science* (forthcoming 2019).

160   **their contributions**: Melissa de Witte, "Instead of 'Finding Your Passion,' Try Developing It, Stanford Scholars Say," *Stanford News*, June 18, 2018. Retrieved from https://news.stanford. edu/2018/06/18/find-passion-may-bad-advice.

161   **interest development**: Suzanne Hidi and K. Ann Renniger, "The Four-Phase Model of Interest Development," *Educational Psychologist*, 2006. Retrieved from https://pdfs.semanticscholar.org/2d90 /b943472c5515730a41ae7f91c69098e61f02.pdf?z_ga=2.88576799 .507060381.1535242406-1936390000.1535242406.

164   **their family**: "Peace, Love, Puppies." Retrieved from https://www.dogdoordogdont.org/about-me.

164   **as girls**: "CNN Young Wonder: Sidney Keys III," CNN, Dec. 12, 2015. Retrieved from www.cnn.com/videos/tv/2017/12/15 /cnnheroes-keys-young-wonder-orig.cnn/video/playlists/2017 -top-10-cnn-heroes.

165   **transform themselves**: Retrieved from www.imagiroo.com/about.

165   **make a difference**: Contributed by Abby Williams, October 6, 2018.

Chapter 12

173   **source of stress**: Fariba Pourjali and Maryam Zarnaghash, "Relationships Between Assertiveness and the Power of Saying No With Mental Health Among Undergraduate Students," *Procedia – Social and Behavioral Sciences*, 2010. Retrieved from www.sciencedirect .com/science/article/pii/S1877042810022317.

173   **assertive by others**: Lorna Collier, "Stand Up For Yourself," *gradPSYCH Magazine*, November 2014. Retrieved from www.apa.org/gradpsych/2014/11/stand-up.aspx.

174   **rights of others**: Pourjali and Zarnaghash, "Relationships Between Assertiveness and the Power of Saying No With Mental Health Among Undergraduate Students."

175   **what we say to others**: Collier, "Stand Up For Yourself."

178   **my community**: Contributed by Andrea Valverde Hernandez.

179 **Grace Warnock**: Iian Gray, "Grace's Sign," Facebook. Retrieved from www.facebook.com/iaingrayeastlothian/videos/9907857 67653198/UzpfSTk2Njc2MzU4MzM4MjUwNToxMDU2NDU zOTI0NDEzNDcw/?fref=ts.

180 **black girls' stories mattered**: Marley Dias, *Marley Dias Gets It Done and So Can You!* (New York: Scholastic, 2018).

180 **useful idea**: Maggie McGrath, "From Activist to Author: How 12-Year-Old Marley Dias Is Changing the Face of Children's Literature," *Forbes*, June 13, 2017. Retrieved from www.forbes.com /sites/maggiemcgrath/2017/06/13/from-activist-to-author-how -12-year-old-marley-dias-is -changing-the-face-of-childrens-literature/#7b43080d4ce0.

181 **run with it, and it can do wonders**: "Pink Shirt Day," CKNW Children's Charities. Retrieved from www.pinkshirtday.ca/about.

184 **possible ways**: Contributed by Matthew Morris, August 23, 2018.